Incentive Compensation
and Employee Ownership
SIXTH EDITION

Incentive Compensation
and Employee Ownership
SIXTH EDITION

Edited by Scott S. Rodrick

The National Center for Employee Ownership
Oakland, California

This publication is designed to provide accurate and authoritative information regarding the subject matter covered. It is sold with the understanding that the publisher is not engaged in rendering legal, accounting, or other professional services. If legal advice or other expert assistance is required, the services of a competent professional should be sought.

Legal, accounting, and other rules affecting business often change. Before making decisions based on the information you find here or in any publication from any publisher, you should ascertain what changes might have occurred and what changes might be forthcoming. The NCEO's Web site (including the members-only area) and newsletter for members provide regular updates on these changes. If you have any questions or concerns about a particular issue, check with your professional advisor or, if you are an NCEO member, call or email us.

Incentive Compensation and Employee Ownership, 6th ed.
Editing and book design by Scott S. Rodrick

Copyright © 2006 by The National Center for Employee Ownership. All rights reserved. No part of this book may be reproduced or transmitted in any form or by any means, electronic or mechanical, including photocopying, recording, or by any information storage and retrieval system, without prior written permission from the publisher.

The National Center for Employee Ownership
1736 Franklin Street, 8th Floor, Oakland, CA 94612
(510) 208-1300
(510) 272-9510 (fax)
Email: *nceo@nceo.org*
Web site: *http://www.nceo.org/*

First edition (under the title *Incentive Compensation for Employee Ownership Companies*) published 1998; second edition, 1998; third edition, 1999; fourth edition, 2002; fifth edition, 2004; sixth edition, 2006.

ISBN: 1-932924-23-X

Contents

Preface

This book discusses incentive compensation—i.e., compensation in the form of a reward for improved individual, group, or company performance. Such plans, which may range from cash bonuses to stock options, form a vital part of the business practices of many companies. In today's competitive business environment, more and more companies are finding that more and more employees are crucial to overall corporate performance; consequently, many of these companies are using incentive compensation to retain employees and encourage them to increase productivity.

Incentive plans relate to employee ownership (i.e., ownership of company stock by employees) in two ways. First, the incentive plan itself may be in the form of stock, in which case it frequently takes the form of a stock option, restricted stock or other such plan (see, e.g., chapter 5, "Restricted Stock Plans"). Second, the short-term rewards of incentive compensation can fill a gap left by a longer-term benefit such as an employee stock ownership plan (ESOP) (see, e.g., the discussion in chapter 2 under the heading "Do Short-Term Incentives Make Ownership Real?").

Although this book covers specific plans at various points (as in chapter 5), it is not a book about restricted stock, stock options, or any other plan per se. Rather, the focus is on the incentive concept and what you can do with it. Other books, such as our publications *The Stock Options Book, Beyond Stock Options,* and many others, describe all the technicalities of particular types of plans. The diversity of plans described in these pages matches the diversity of plans you will find in various companies. It is common to find more than one type of stock or cash incentive plan, as with the ESOP companies profiled in chapter 2 that also use short-term incentives.

Readers should recognize that what works for one situation may not work for another, but that at the same time meaningless, feel-good slogans about empowering employees will not fill the bill. An effective incentive plan needs to be specific and customized for each particular situation. You probably will not find an exact blueprint for your company's plan in the following pages; you will, however, find a wealth of information, ideas, and inspiration on how to proceed. We hope that some of these ideas will fit your situation or, more likely, will stimulate you to think of some new combinations of ideas that will work.

The chapters in this book fall into two basic categories. First, the chapters in Part One, "Essays," introduce readers to the field of incentive compensation and describe how various plans, both stock- and cash-based, operate in general terms. Second, the chapters in Part Two, "Case Studies," illustrate how specific companies have implemented specific plans.

Sixth Edition (2006)

The sixth edition has been revised to clarify the technical material and bring it up-to-date (as in the discussion of accounting and deferred compensation rules in chapter 4, or at various points in chapters 5); to fine-tune the chapter on cash incentives (chapter 8); to update the case studies on Apex Systems and Intuit; and to add a case study on TEOCO, The Employee Owned Company (chapter 14). The SAIC case study (chapter 10 in the fifth edition) was removed because changes at SAIC made the chapter outdated, while pending changes make it unfeasible to revise at this time.

Part One
Essays

Measuring, Improving, and Rewarding Performance

Jerry McAdams

It has taken us 80 years since the Industrial Revolution to discover the customer and about 90 to discover employees. And discover them we have. We have figured out how to calculate the lifetime value of a customer and are trying to figure out the value of employee contributions to the success of our organizations. Just how important employees are to the company is being brought home to us through this book. It provides us with practices that have been developed and tested, practices that are making a difference.

Use Every Asset You Have

Competitiveness demands getting the best possible return on an organization's assets. If you believe people are assets and not solely a cost of doing business, this book shows you ways of getting a better return on these employed assets. In addition to base pay, many organizations are spending a good deal of money, time, and energy on all kinds of compensation, reward, and recognition plans

---

Mr. McAdams adapted portions of this chapter from his book *The Reward Plan Advantage: A Manager's Guide to Improving Business Performance Through People* (San Francisco, CA: Jossey-Bass, 1996).

with little understanding of what they are getting back. If they try to understand what they get back, sometimes they can put a dollar value on their return. Sometimes they can't. (It may make good business sense even without a dollar return.) In either case, when organizations want employees to make a difference, they must be clear on their objectives and make the plans *positively reinforcing* to employees. In addition, if we want to maximize that return, organizations must have the courage to unleash the creative energy of employees, enabling them to become contributing stakeholders. This process of involving employees as contributing stakeholders is being successfully applied in every type of organization—service, manufacturing, union, non-union, private and public. For many, it is the *way they operate the organization*.

The Reinforcement Model

Most of us have a basic understanding of how pay systems work. We are probably not going to change the fundamental way we pay people. Therefore, the focus is on a better understanding of what we get from these systems now and how we can use additional (or redirected) funds to launch plans more directly aligned with your organization's objectives.

It is helpful to put these plans in context through a reinforcement model (figure 1-1). *Business Objectives and Desired Culture* drive the design of reinforcement systems, characterized as *compensation, capability, recognition, group incentive,* and *project team incentive* plans. These characterizations are ordered from left to right in figure 1-1 according to their contribution to results—the degree to which one can attribute performance improvement to the plan. The two ends of the continuum are labeled "cost of doing business"—*compensation* (base pay, benefits, and most adjustments to base pay)—and "business results"—*project team incentive* plans that reward only when the result of the contribution is measurable and valuable. The more one moves from left to right, the more directly one can attribute the business result to the reward plan.

Moving from left to right also moves from an administrative mindset to a creative one. Beginning at *capability* plans, the creative

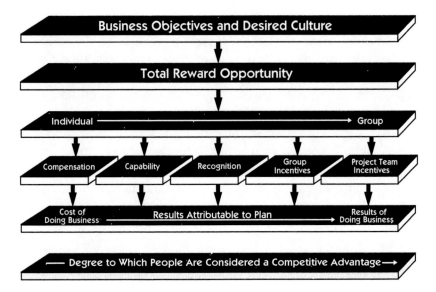

Figure 1-1. The reinforcement model

demand from an organization focuses on imaginative approaches in a constantly changing environment. It describes an increasing opportunity for alignment between all employees and those objectives that determine organizational success. It deals with the ability of an organization to meet those objectives in a cost-effective manner. It can open up the systems to allow employees to move from job-bound, narrowly focused, micro-managed cost centers to enabled corporate contributors with both accountability and reward. Issues of goal setting; coaching and feedback; performance appraisal; and pay for knowledge, skill, and competencies are those of *capability*.

Recognition as the Organizationally Approved "Thank You"

Recognition plans are after the fact, by definition. They are not "do this and you will get that," but "we saw you do this and thanks for doing it." Whenever possible, think as recognition as the WD-40 oil of all interventions. It smoothes the way for all performance improvement by creating and reinforcing an environment of positive consequences for positive behavior and results. Recognition is most effective when it is not competitive. Organizational objectives are rarely met by employees competing for a limited number of awards; rather, they are met by employees cooperating in the best interests of all.

In any case, recognition must be done with honesty and sincerity. It can be public or private. It can be of significant or symbolic value. It can recognize individuals or groups. It can come from management or peers. It is highly flexible, able to be changed from month to month, objective to objective. But it always must be honest and sincere.

Improvement by Adding a Group Focus

Most managers have been taught to believe that proper administration of compensation plans is their only weapon and that it can (or should) do it all. I disagree.

We already know a good deal about improving performance by focusing on the individual employee. This practice assumes that improvement of every person's performance (assuming one could measure it) will roll up to organizational improvement. While that may be the case, we will never know for sure if it works. With the possible exception of sales, we cannot prove that a 10% improvement in individual productivity, as an example, will result in a cumulative 10% productivity gain for the entire organization—or any gain at all, for that matter. Accounting, measurement, job, and operational systems are too complex for such a simplistic approach.

Competitiveness demands engaging all employees in making a business successful. That demands that everyone know, understand, focus, and act on those objectives that determine organizational success. Group incentive and project team incentive plans, in the broadest terms, are designed expressly to improve organizational success.

At a conference in San Francisco, one of my audience members argued against rewarding everyone in a group for improving performance. He didn't believe a file clerk could influence the measures. I pointed out he was right—-if you just see the person as a file clerk, confined to filing. But if you view the clerk as an intelligent human being and allow him or her to contribute, he could make a difference. Our challenge is to enable that file clerk to collaborate with others to make a contribution and be rewarded for the result or recognized for the effort.

Group incentives are distinguished from project team incentives by the definition of "group." In this case, it means an organizational unit—a workgroup, department, division, business unit, or entire company. A project team does not appear on the organizational chart. It can be two people in the same workgroup or a cross-functional team assembled for a specific purpose. In either the group or project team incentive plans, the focus is on results of the group or team and not on individual contributions. Mixing the focus reduces the effectiveness of the plans. You can have plans designed specifically for individuals that work nicely along the side of group or team-based plans.

An additional goal of these plans is to create an environment that unleashes the creativity of employees. That creativity, when channeled through clear direction and enabling processes, is one of our most effective competitive elements.

It's Not All About Reinforcement

I do not believe that individual compensation, recognition, and reward plans are the *only* way to improve an organization's performance. Far from it. Financial literacy, organizational redesign, re-engineering, systems and process development, new products and services, quality, becoming "customer-driven," along with hiring, orientation, and career development practices and all kinds of other interventions are destined to affect performance.

Reinforcement systems can lead the improvement process or lag it, but they absolutely must reinforce it. The problem is that most experts in these other disciplines mentioned in the paragraph above only pay lip service to reinforcement, and that is a lost opportunity. Those of us who have participated in our umpteenth management by objective (MBO) process, without reinforcement, know what I mean. I believe what gets measured gets managed, and what gets rewarded gets done.

Another caveat: I believe in intrinsic rewards as well as extrinsic. We need both. No reward plan will offset a lousy supervisor who makes your job painful. Nor will it offset a job you hate. By the same token, to rely solely on intrinsic rewards is a mistake. It doesn't take long for employees to say, "I really like working on this special team to improve the process, but what else is in it for me?" As with all things, we must strike a balance.

As my father, a tough Depression-age realist, used to say, "If you want to get people really involved, get them to put some skin in the game." In this context, "skin" is employees sharing risk *and* reward with the organization in the game of business.

I suggest that you review the case studies included here as thought-starters and "tales from the trenches." They are not to be replicated but instead adapted to your organizational needs. With the proper use of this information, you can be better prepared to meet the challenges of an increasingly competitive marketplace.

Beyond Bribery: Communicating Short-Term Group Incentives

Cathy Ivancic

"Eat your vegetables and you can have dessert," the old saying goes. Does this extrinsic reward—dessert—really motivate anyone to eat vegetables? I know that my child complies with this "incentive" by jamming the remaining zucchini into his mouth and swallowing hard. I did the same to my parents when they offered me this incentive. (Perhaps you did too.) Obviously, the reward did not create a full understanding of the need for the behavior, nor did it develop a desire to repeat it in the future. No, the "dessert" incentive engendered only temporary compliance, not a real "ownership" of the process.

Creating incentives that encourage an ownership mentality can be a challenge. Employee-owned companies often turn to short-term group incentives to provide current benefits for owners, stimulate a deeper sense of ownership, and build knowledge about the business. But what makes short-term group incentives in employee-owned companies any different from the classic vegetable bribe?

Even incentives implemented for the right reasons can be perceived by employees as meaningless or manipulative. The challenge, of course, is getting beyond bribery. Proper incentive design is a starting point, but the ultimate success of an incentive is rooted in how it is communicated and implemented. This chapter, by describing the experiences of three companies with success in this area and providing specific ideas for improving communication approaches, illustrates how the communication of short-term incentives can enhance their effectiveness.

Do Short-Term Incentives Make Ownership Real?

Employee ownership's greatest strength—a shared interest in long-term performance—is also its greatest weakness. For younger employees and people who are not familiar with the benefits of equity ownership, the rewards can seem nonexistent. Equity ownership has drawbacks as an incentive. First, the rewards are not timely, and second, the connection to daily work is difficult to see. This is particularly true where the value of the equity is realized at retirement, such as in an employee stock ownership plan (ESOP). In ESOP companies, incentives are frequently implemented to make ownership more "real." If you reward people for current performance results, so the thinking goes, they will be more aware of how the business is doing and pay attention to performance.

Among the strongest advocates of short-term incentives are companies that describe themselves as "open-book" firms. These companies point to their bonus programs as linchpins of their successful approach.[1] Open-book advocate Jack Stack, president of Springfield ReManufacturing Corporation, summed it up this way: "What a bonus program does is communicate goals in the most effective way possible—by putting a bounty on them."[2]

But this positive experience with incentives is not universal. In fact, many employee-owned companies are disappointed with the results of their incentive programs. The story often goes something like this: XYZ company has an annual bonus tied to performance such as a percentage of annual net income. In addition, employees also have the long-term benefit of employee ownership. Despite these clear incentives, people do not act in ways that earn the bonus or grow stock value. Leaders at XYZ company have posted reports and provided information on the incentive with little results from the apathetic work force. Like children who resist eating vegetables, the employee owners do not know what is good for them.

Research on rewards supports this notion that rewards can backfire and fail to cultivate an understanding of group purpose. The critics of incentives—including leading organizational thinkers such as W. Edwards Deming—say that rewards can encourage short-term thinking, nourish rivalries, and even damage teamwork.[3] These negative analyses are most strongly targeted at individual merit pay-for-performance plans, but critiques are also leveled against group incentives such as profit sharing plans and group bonus systems. Rosabeth Moss Kanter notes that variable incentives are often unconnected to what employees contribute and may put a large part of compensation at risk—a problem for lower-paid employees who cannot afford to take that chance.[4] In *Punished by Rewards*, Alfie Kohn characterizes incentives as manipulations that cultivate shortsighted behavior, encourage orchestration of appearances, and distract from the intrinsic value of doing good work. Kohn argues that even group rewards can muster only "temporary compliance" and will eventually be seen as manipulation.[5] Peter Block contends—in his 1993 critique of traditional corporate governance—that despite the popular belief to the contrary, the research on rewards indicates that "productivity is not for sale."[6]

Designing Group Incentives

Many problems with group incentives result from one or more of the following design flaws, which inhibit the plan's effectiveness:

- Incentives create too much focus on one goal (e.g., production) at the expense of another (e.g., quality).
- Incentives reward the wrong behavior for the objectives of the plan.
- They are discretionary (at a supervisor or board's discretion).
- The plan is too complex for the group's level of knowledge.
- The incentive is not calculated frequently enough (monthly is better than annually).

- The payment does not vary.
- The plan rewards individual performance, thereby creating competition where teamwork is needed.
- The incentive is not tied to company-wide performance.
- Employee efforts are not connected to the reward.
- The incentive is not self-funding.

A challenge of incentive design is the fact that there are necessary tradeoffs. When a plan is simple and tied to company-wide goals, it is often not clearly related to things employees control. On the other hand, an incentive linked to department or team performance, which is easy to understand, may miss the mark regarding the company's general performance. When incentives are tied to a purely objective calculation, they may not take into account subjective measures that are important for the future success of the company. Because of these tradeoffs, the search for the perfect incentive formula can be a futile one. In fact, many of the companies that describe their incentives as outstanding successes technically suffer from one or more of the above design flaws.

Attention to design can avoid creating insurmountable obstacles, but the success of group incentives ultimately rests on the effectiveness of the processes used to implement and communicate them. Good design cannot overcome poor communication, but good communication can overcome flaws caused by tradeoffs in the design process.

Communicating Short-Term Incentives

The three employee-owned companies highlighted in this chapter describe their incentive programs as a 6 or higher on a scale of 1 to 10 in terms of reaching their intended objectives.[7] The design elements of these successful short-term incentives vary tremendously, but the communication of the plans have the following common characteristics. Each of the three companies found a way for the incentive to be "owned" by employees, linked it to growing knowledge of business objectives, and created ways for people to make improvements in the business.

Bimba Manufacturing: Keeping Track and Growing Knowledge of "Our" Business

"I don't do my job to get the bonus. I'm from the old school where you are expected to do a good job. The bonus just helps me know how well we are doing," says Brian Cash, a maintenance leader at Bimba Manufacturing in Monee, Illinois. Similarly, his coworker Joyce Greep explains that she will gladly accept higher performance goals "because I'm proud of my company and want to serve customers." For Greep and Cash, the incentive is an indicator of how *their company* is doing rather than an exercise in satisfying company leaders. This buy-in by employees—achieved more by implementation than by design—is an essential ingredient in the success of a group incentive.

The objectives of the Bimba incentive plan are to broaden the understanding of customer requirements, share rewards, and build a sense of purpose. "We have a written vision statement, but the incentives reinforce our purpose and keep the focus," notes Dennis Damrow, vice president of operations at the employee-owned manufacturer of pneumatic actuators.

Group incentives for the 450 employee owners at Bimba Manufacturing come in several forms. The company calculates a quarterly bonus based on exceeding performance targets. When targets are exceeded, everyone in the company can earn up to 10% of compensation in a bonus. Sixty percent of that amount is contingent on company-wide profitability targets. The other 40% is contingent on reaching specific workgroup targets. The workgroup targets focus on the specific function of a department. For example, a department may have local targets related to customer service, work order completion, and safety. In order for someone in that department to get their full bonus, the company-wide target and the local targets must be met.

Bonus payments have been generated often, but they are not

guaranteed. For example, two years ago the program paid in only two of the four quarters. Last year there were payments every quarter.

In addition to the bonus described above, Bimba has a separate customer service bonus that can be paid quarterly. This bonus—a flat $250 per person—is contingent on meeting targets on product request dates and promise dates. The company recently initiated a new way of tracking this bonus. Rather than paying $250 when the summarized quarterly targets are met, the targets are tracked weekly. When each weekly target is met, $20 is added to that quarter's customer service bonus.

Company leaders and employees agree that the incentives have contributed to improved performance. Bimba has significantly outpaced the industry in volume growth. In addition, the company received Class A MRP-II (customer service) certification in January 1996. The bonus program's most significant effect has been to focus a greater number of people on customer requirements. Customer service targets have been increased in each of the past four years, with current targets at 97% of promise dates and 90% of request dates.

Incentives are communicated in a variety of ways at Bimba. The company makes use of conventional communication methods, including annual meetings, newsletters, and posting of results. Departments select their own methods to share results, including postings, meetings, and one-on-one conversations.

Bimba also makes use of some uncommon approaches. The incentives are included in the company's week-long orientation for new employees. It is one of the 16 different sessions provided. New employees also learn about benefits, the company's markets, diversity, problem-solving, and the company's ESOP. The message for new employees is clear: these incentives are part of this company's overall business strategy, and it is very important that everyone in the company understand that strategy.

The ongoing tracking and communication of the customer service measure takes place weekly. Each Monday a cross-functional group of managers and schedulers meets to review the week's performance. The meeting, run by the sales and marketing department, provides current information to the rest of the company about performance on customer service targets. The information in the Monday meeting is brought back to each workgroup. Weekly tracking reveals the effect that events and different departments have on the numbers. The way local targets are set is also part of the communication process.

Setting local targets is an exercise in helping people connect their department to the company's objectives. Leaders in each department are asked to identify the things they do in their area that help reach the company-wide goals. They make a proposal, and the departmental activities are turned into targets that quantify their connection, with guidance from top-level leaders. The process of talking about and setting targets is an education for everyone involved on how all the pieces fit together to meet company goals. "That (the communication about goals) is the real benefit," according to Damrow.

On the surface, the Bimba Manufacturing incentives seem complex and difficult to understand. However, in the context of how the incentive evolved, it becomes clear that current incentives are the result of a multi-year educational process. Today's bonuses came about as company leaders changed the incentive each year to fit with current objectives and the growing sophistication of employee owners.

Each modification helped people to learn about new elements of their business. When the company first established the ESOP, discretionary bonuses were paid. Looking for a better link to performance, the quarterly incentive was established in 1989. The first incentive bonus was simple; it was paid if the company as a whole exceeded profitability targets. A few years later, the customer service measures were included as part of the company-wide goals. In the following year, the customer service incentive was broken out as a separate bonus paid equally to each person, and the other bonus remained a percentage of pay. In recent years, the local incentives were added as part of the criteria for the bonus based on compensation.

In this evolutionary context, Bimba's local incentives are reflections of the overall company goals rather than distinct departmental rewards. The two-way conversation about how each work area contributes to the company's goals connects local incentives to the common goals. "It works like a relay team," says Greep, "If we find they [workers in another department] aren't making their bonus, we'll figure out how we can pass the baton better to help them get it."

The range of incentives and the changing targets at Bimba Manufacturing help people learn more about their company and what helps improve its performance. The two-way communication about targets and the frequency of that communication have created incentives that are tools for continuous improvement rather than carrots for behavior.

Zandex: Employee Owners Create Their Own Incentive

"I like to describe it as the 'birthing process,'" says Kurt Southam, president of Zandex Health Care Corporation, when talking about employee participation in developing incentives. At this Ohio chain of nursing and retirement homes, nearly 1,000 employees had opportunities to comment, critique, and modify a proposed incentive plan. This "gestation period," according to Southam, helped people to support the end result. In a sense, the long process of feedback and redraft helped make the incentives their "baby."

One of the Zandex incentives—the Committed Owners of Zandex program (COZ)—creates a special set of rewards for employees who are committed to the company mission. The company's mission, which was developed several years before the incentive plan, is "to provide compassionate, responsible care for residents which will provide security for the employees and profitability for the shareholders." At Zandex, employees are shareholders, with 25% of the shares in an ESOP.

The COZ program came about as a result of discussions initiated by company leaders about the obstacles to accomplishing the company's mission. One of the obstacles employee owners identified was the lack of a way to reward people who consistently supported the company's mission.

All employees were asked to comment in writing and in small groups on the best way to reward these "exceptional people" and also to help develop criteria for selecting who these people are. The rewards selected were extra personal days, vacation days, an automatic attendance bonus, and an extra grade at the top of the pay scale. There were five rounds of comments and ideas collected from employees on various drafts of the proposed program. A high percentage of employees shared ideas on the plan.

Through this process, employees selected the criteria for who was a "committed owner." A COZ employee is judged on the following criteria: attendance, flexibility, initiative, professionalism, teamwork, company commitment, and grooming. To become eligible for the program, an employee is recommended by his or her supervisor and required to pass a short test about company policies and employee ownership. The test is changed each year. If an employee's performance has remained good, he or she is invited to take another version of the test on company philosophy and policies to enter the program again.

The COZ program was put to a vote by each of the company's eight locations. Employee owners voted in proportion to the shares in their ESOP accounts (participants with no shares were given five votes). All but one location passed the final proposal by an 80% positive vote. The program was implemented in all facilities except for that one location. Employee owners at this facility sent a clear message that—at the time of the vote—this incentive was not "their baby." Later that year, employees of that facility voted to have the COZ program (90% wanted it).

After one year of the program, approximately 40% of employees are COZ employees. This program, along with the other incentives at Zandex, has contributed to cutting absenteeism in half and significantly reducing turnover.

Zandex has used this process of employee commentary to arrive at policies on company issues and incentives. Voting on nearly all policy changes, employee owners at Zandex have a direct say in changes that directly affect their work life.

The company has a bonus based on company profitability that is paid every six months. Three years ago, the company proposed to reduce the bonus checks of people with excessive "call-offs" (absenteeism resulting from the employee calling in sick or with an excuse); attendance is a recurring problem in this industry, where the jobs are emotionally challenging and turnover is high. Employees voted on both the number of acceptable "call offs" and later on whether it would result in a reduction or a complete forfeiture of the bonus. The group voted to have employees who have excessive "call offs" forfeit their bonus completely and reallocate that money to other employees.

Without the "birthing process," these incentive programs can resemble the kind of reward critics say will create divisions and erode teamwork. The programs make distinctions between individuals based on merit, and COZ has subjective judgment by supervisors. But the employees themselves said that such distinctions were necessary to support Zandex's mission. Through the process, employees tinkered with the program to help minimize its design tradeoffs and still accomplish its objectives. Employee owners came to "own" the incentive by having a chance to shape it.

Floturn: Awareness Through Formal and Informal Communication

When you come to work at Floturn, an employee-owned manufacturer in Cincinnati, Ohio, you need to understand the bonus system to take the job. Without understanding it, you will not know whether you are being compensated adequately. Base pay is typically just below market rates at this manufacturer of laser printer and photocopier substrates. It is the bonus program that makes it a good-paying job. The bonus, which has been in existence since 1971, typically pays anywhere from 75% to 125% of annual compensation each year.

The bonus pool is one-third of company profits. "One-third goes to the bonus pool, one-third goes back into the company, and one-third goes to taxes," explains Art Scharinger, company treasurer. The annualized bonus is paid on a quarterly basis. The pool is paid to employee owners as a percentage of compensation. In early quarters, a percentage of the quarterly calculation is reserved to offset the possibility of poor performance in future quarters. By the end of the year, the full one-third of profits is paid out.

Floturn consistently pays bonuses. "There was only one year, 1986, when we didn't pay any bonus," says Scharinger. The amounts of the bonuses, however, vary with company performance, from as low as 6.5% of pay in the early years to well over 100% in recent years.

Company officials feel that the company's ESOP, which owns more than 80% of the company's stock, provides a hedge against shortsighted thinking that might be created by this kind of incentive. The bonus is designed to work with the ESOP, providing short-term gains for employee owners who will not realize equity (i.e., ESOP) benefits until retirement.

The bonus has helped to build awareness about company performance and help people understand how everyday work affects it. For example, a machine operator pointed out that moving another machine closer to his workstation would enable him to run two machines simultaneously. "Without the bonus, we would not have seen that kind of awareness, " noted Scharinger. This awareness is combined with a management style that assumes that people can make improvements in the business and encourages them to do so.

As a result of the business awareness, people have made corrections that have reduced costs, such as reducing scrap and cutting back the hours they work. These efforts—combined with a fast-growing market—have led to outstanding corporate performance. Floturn's stock value has increased more than 1,080% in less than an eight-year period. The company has outperformed the industry in growth. When the industry grew 16%, Floturn grew 30%.

Communication about the bonus program starts before you even work at Floturn. It begins with your first introduction to the company, which is likely to be from a family member who works there. Exposure to information about the bonus continues through employee orientation and quarterly meetings about the bonus. Each quarter the company has a meeting where the financial results are shared and the bonus is announced. The meeting is on paid time. Each month of the quarter there is some communication about the bonus; in the first month there is the quarterly meeting, a month later people get the check, and the following month the next quarter closes.

On top of the formal communication, there are many informal ways people learn about how they affect business performance. When the company first became employee-owned, only a small group of 33 people worked at the facility. With the small size and a relatively flat organization, the company established a tradition of leaders responding to questions about performance and helping people see the connection to their jobs.

As the company grows (it now employs nearly 140 people), informal communication continues to be an important part of how people learn about the business. "Most people are related to someone here," says Scharinger. "Old-timers tell the newcomers how our work affects the bonus." In addition, because such a large part of compensation is tied to performance, employees may have to explain the bonus to people outside the company. For example, the company helps employees explain the compensation system to lenders when employee owners want to buy a house.

While some companies achieve their educational objectives by changing the bonus, Floturn has instead achieved an educational impact by keeping it the same. The longevity of the bonus, the regularized communication, and the size of the payouts has created an incentive system that is well known and valued by employee owners.

An Incentive People Can Call Their Own

Employee ownership companies may have an advantage over conventionally owned companies because the long-term benefit of equity ownership balances short-term thinking created by an incentive plan. Ownership may create a foundation for seeing the incentive as a step toward a shared goal rather than a manipulative practice. As Frank Hudetz, the CEO of Solar Press, an employee-owned company in Naperville, Illinois, writes, "long-term incentives tied to company philosophy can prove worthy of the highest employee performance and build intrinsic motivation—the highest order of incentive."[8]

Most of the research suggests that employee ownership alone, without employee participation, does not create this "highest order of incentive."[9] In companies like those described above, the implementation and communication of the short-term incentives are key elements in effective participation. Properly communicated and implemented incentives provide a focus for working toward common goals.

The companies in this chapter have not discovered the perfect group incentive formula. Each incentive has its design tradeoffs. Bimba Manufacturing is an elaborate plan that can be complex to understand. Zandex's COZ program relies on subjective measures that could be seen as favoritism. Floturn's bonus based on profitability is not tied directly to job-level improvements. If you took any one of these incentive designs and transplanted them into another company, the incentive would have a high likelihood of failure. Design is not the common denominator in their success. It is the way they have implemented the design that makes them work.

Each of the companies uses a communication process in which the methods and the tone send a strong message about who is in charge of the incentive. The incentive is not perceived by employees as management's effort to change their behavior; instead, it is a scorecard to show people how they are doing. In addition, these companies are clear about how the incentive fits with the group's shared objectives. The specific communication processes chosen are different, but they have following common characteristics:

Employees, not company leaders, "own" the process. When people talk about group incentives in these companies, they describe it as something the group can influence. The incentive is not a reward bestowed on employees by leaders or a carrot to motivate employees. Leaders do not dish out the rewards. Instead, it is a way of keeping track of shared performance.

Incentives are part of building knowledge about business objectives. Successful group incentives are not stand-alone programs, they are expressions of business objectives. These incentives find their way into regularized communications, formal education sessions, and informal dialogue about work. These incentives are part of reaching common objectives and learning how to do that better. One of their key functions is to teach people about how the company makes money.

People get more than material rewards. Social and emotional rewards come from the fact that people are empowered to affect results. Working together to achieve the reward, using one's creativity to solve problems, and being a part of reaching objectives are personally rewarding. The way an incentive is implemented can help or hinder its ability to generate these nonmaterial rewards for people.

Methods to Help Improve Communication About Group Incentives

Identifying these common characteristics of success is not a useful exercise without practical ideas about the actions that help create these results. What can companies do to improve their communication about incentives? The ideas below, based on the experiences of more than 50 employee-owned companies throughout the United States that use incentives, can provide a starting point for companies working to improve their communication about incentives.[10]

Include both numbers and the stories behind the numbers. Develop the skills of leaders throughout your company to communicate about performance in both numbers and stories. Group incentives tied to measurable results are not useful if people do not understand how the measure fits with daily work. Stories paint the picture of how work and the performance numbers fit together. The art of telling the business story must be cultivated throughout the company.

Provide an opportunity for people at all levels to tell their own stories. Top-level leaders need to work to relinquish the job of explaining why the incentive went up or down. Employees must to develop the knowledge and information needed to be able to tell their own stories. Leaders should challenge them to do this by turning the communication about performance into a two-way conversation and creating regular opportunities for the conversation to take place. If your company chooses to do formal training on business concepts, make sure the educational approach goes beyond a standard lecture-style format and challenges people to practice talking about their contribution to performance.

Run communication on a frequent and regular schedule. If an employee only hears about the bonus at the annual meeting, it is difficult to see the connection to daily work. Regularized communications (quarterly, monthly, or even weekly) help make the incentive a point of focus for daily activities. Moreover, they provide the repetition needed for learning to take place.

Educate people on how their work affects the numbers. Teach people about how they affect performance. Teaching about company financial statements is not enough. Focus educational efforts—both those that happen in a classroom and regularized company communications—on creating a "line of sight" (i.e., a clearly perceptible connection) between daily work and company performance. Developing a common language for talking about these connections is much more important than knowledge of financial statements.

Set objectives for your incentive and invite employees to participate in the process. If there are not clear goals for the incentive plan, it is time to think again about whether one is needed. Asking employees to help define the goals of the incentive, set the criteria, or establish local objectives helps people "own" the results.

Create opportunities for employees to make improvements that affect performance. Without avenues for employee participation, an incentive cannot be a way to focus actions. Consider the following approaches to excessive overtime. One approach is to set a company limit on available overtime and explain that it is in everyone's interest because it is eating into the bonus. A second approach would be to explain how overtime is connected to the bonus and challenge employees to make suggestions and implement changes in the things that contribute to excessive overtime. In the first example, the incentive is a justification for a company policy. In the second example, the incentive is evidence that employees can affect performance. A group incentive is empty without genuine empowerment to make improvements.

Make it fun and engaging. Who made the rule that communication about company performance must be boring and dull? Most of the traditional means for communicating about performance—annual reports, shareholder meetings, or reviews of the financial statements—were originally designed for outsiders. Meeting targets is fun; overcoming business challenges is exciting; working together toward common goals is rewarding. Unfortunately, most companies do not make their communication about these things reflect that excitement. When communicating with insiders, it is fine to break the "rules" by making it into a game, using visual aids and props, making noise, singing, or even jumping up on your chair. Consider that communicating about performance is not much different from other ways of keeping score for a group. An announcer at a football game would never say, "on page six of the handout you'll see the detailed graph that shows Central High has improved yards gained in the second quarter." Keep score on a big board where everyone can see and get employee owners involved in providing the high-energy commentary.

Beyond Bribery: Who Owns the Results in Your Company?

Short-term group incentives do not always develop a sense of purpose or an "ownership" of the work process. The implementation and communication of group incentives can make a tremendous difference in whether employee owners see the incentive as manipulation—like the "vegetable bribe"—or as a tool for self-improvement. When employee owners believe that leaders are in control of the game (as in a parent-child relationship), incentives will create temporary compliance at best. When employee owners do not understand their business and its objectives, incentives cannot help achieve the business objectives. Finally, unless extrinsic incentives help people to track and control their own activities, the reward will not help people to take "ownership" of the results of their work.

Notes

1. See John Case, *Open-Book Management: The Coming Business Revolution*, (New York: HarperCollins, 1995), and John P. Schuster, Jill Carpenter, and M. Patricia Kane, *The Power of Open-Book Management* (New York: John Wiley & Sons, Inc., 1996) for detailed examples of companies that describe the incentive component of their company culture as an important element of their success.

2. Jack Stack and Bo Burlingham, *The Great Game of Business* (New York: Currency Doubleday, 1992), 122. [Editor's note: The relevant chapter in Stack's book is excerpted in chapter 3 of this book.]

3. W. Edwards Deming, *Out of the Crisis* (Cambridge: MIT Center for Advanced Engineering Study, 1986), 102. See also Fredrick Herzberg, "One More Time: How Do You Motivate Employees?" *Harvard Business Review*, January/February 1968, 53–62. Herzberg maintains the answer to this question is that "you don't."

4. See Rosabeth Moss Kanter, *When Giants Learn to Dance* (New York: Simon and Schuster, 1989), 234–237.

5. Alfie Kohn, *Punished by Rewards: The Trouble with Gold Stars, Incentive Plans, A's, Praise, and Other Bribes* (New York: Houghton Mifflin Company, 1993).

6. See Peter S. Block, *Stewardship: Choosing Service over Self-Interest* (San Francisco: Berrett Koehler Publishers, 1993), 167.

7. Descriptions are based on conversations with company leaders and formal interviews completed in fall 1996.

8. See Frank C. Hudetz," Self-Actualization and Self-Esteem Are the Highest Order of Incentives," at the Foundation for Enterprise Development's World Wide Web site at *http://www.fed.org/*.

9. Employee ownership alone is not correlated with improved corporate performance. See General Accounting Office, *Employee Ownership Plans: Little Evidence of Effects on Corporate Performance* (Washington, D.C.: GAO/PEMD-88-1, 1987).

10. See Cathy Ivancic and Jim Bado, *Open-Book Management: Getting Started* (Menlo Park, CA: Crisp Publications, 1997).

Incentive Compensation and the Great Game of Business

Jack Stack

There is no more powerful tool a manager can have than a good bonus program—which is why some companies will pay a consultant tens of thousands of dollars to design one. That's not necessarily a stupid investment. If a bonus program works, it can be an incredible motivator. It can get people producing at levels that make the cost of the program seem like peanuts, no matter how much you may have spent to set it up.

What a bonus program does is communicate goals in the most effective way possible—by putting a bounty on them. It says to people, "These targets are so important, we'll give you a reward if you hit them." When you do that, you get people's attention very fast. You send them a strong message. You provide them with a focus. You give them a challenge and a very good reason for working as hard and as smart as they can to meet it: they're going to get paid. In "the Great Game of Business" (the "Game"), we get all that and much, much more from our bonus program, and we didn't pay anyone a dime to come up with it. We call it "Skip the Praise—

Mr. Stack adapted this chapter from his and Bo Burlingham's book *The Great Game of Business* (New York: Currency Books, 1992), chapter 7, "Skip The Praise—Give Us the Raise."

Give Us the Raise," or STP-GUTR—pronounced Stop-Gooter. Following are some of the things we like about it.

Stop-Gooter is our most effective educational program. We use it to teach people about business. If the goal is to improve the debt-equity ratio, people learn about debt and equity and how they affect both. The same holds for pretax profits, or inventory accuracy, or the overhead charge-out rate. Whatever the goal, it gives people a big incentive to find out about some aspect of the accounting system, the company, and the competitive environment. Otherwise they won't have much fun, they won't earn the bonus, and they'll take a lot of flak from their peers.

The bonus program serves as a kind of insurance policy on the company and our jobs. That's because we use it to target our vulnerabilities. Every year, we figure out what the greatest threat the company faces is, and we get the entire work force to go after it in the bonus program. In effect, we put an annual bounty on fixing our weaknesses. That gives everyone an additional reason to achieve the goals. These are musts, not wants, and so they are worth the extra effort. Interestingly enough, once a weakness is fixed, it tends to say fixed.

The program brings us together as a team. It ensures that everyone has the same priorities and that we all stay focused on the same goals. It eliminates mixed messages. When one department is having trouble, another department will send in reinforcements, and everybody understands why. Often, people don't even have to be asked. They will help each other out spontaneously, sometimes at great inconvenience. That's because the program makes everyone aware of how much we depend on one another to hit our targets. We win together or we don't win at all.

The program helps us identify problems fast. If we don't achieve a goal, we find out very quickly why we missed it. Everybody is looking through the numbers to see what the problem is. Maybe it's receivables: customers are slowing down their payments and conserving cash. Maybe it's productivity: people are new in their jobs and can't absorb overhead fast enough. The bonus program forces the problem out into the open. Once it's there, you can go to work on it. You can solve it.

Stop-Gooter is the best tool we have for increasing the value of our stock. We always set it up to guarantee the stock value will rise substantially if we hit our targets—and will be protected even if we don't. That's one of the most important messages we send through the program: "This Game is all about equity and job security." Short-term incentives like bonuses are fine, but we want to make sure people never lose sight of the long-term payoff.

Most importantly, the bonus program provides the structure of the Game. It puts the ball in play. It sets the tempo. It keeps the action going week in, week out, all year long. It gives us a language, a way of communicating. It creates excitement, anticipation. It gets the adrenaline flowing. It makes sure that people stay involved, engaged, on their toes. It is, in short, our most important motivator, which is its primary function. If it weren't raising the energy level, we'd stop using it, although I find it hard to imagine how it could fail to motivate. That's a question we constantly pose: "Is the bonus program motivating people?" But I have to admit that if anybody ever told me it wasn't, I'd think that he was a dirty liar—or that our education program was in deep trouble.

Bootstrapping: The Best Reason for Paying People with Bonuses

I am a strong believer in operating a company, any company, as if its future were always on the line, as if something could happen at any moment to threaten its survival. Most companies do, in fact, follow that principle when they are starting up. They don't take the future for granted because they can't. They know that they could run out of cash next week and the game would be over. So they become extremely resourceful. They constantly look for an edge, for ways to cut costs and save money, for things they can do to get more bang for their buck. It's known as bootstrapping, and it's how every business should be run, not just startups. Bootstrapping is a mentality, a set of habits, and a way of operating based on self-reliance, ingenuity, intelligence, and hard work. When you don't bootstrap, you grow fat and sloppy. You get into the habit of buying solutions to your problems. You take the future for granted. You assume you'll be in business forever. You let your costs rise, and you take your eye off the ball. You get caught up in a lot of issues that have nothing to do with making money and generating cash. The next thing you know, a competitor comes along and knocks you out of the box. Suddenly, your company doesn't have much of a future, and you may not have a job.

A good bonus system can help you build a bootstrapping mentality into your organization. It does that by putting a great deal of emphasis on job security by reminding people what it takes to protect their jobs and by showing them how they can get more.

There is only one sure way to protect jobs, and that is to be ruthless about costs. But least-cost companies face an unpleasant choice. If you want to come in below your competitors, you can (1) pay your people less or (2) make your product faster. That's about it. No humane person enjoys making such a choice. Who wants to have a business that provides people with the lowest standard of living in the market or that forces them to work so fast it's unhealthy? Who wants a company that prevents people from taking care of their families and themselves, from leading a full and happy life? But what's the alternative if you're going to be competitive and stay in business?

A bonus system like ours offers a way around this dilemma. It allows the company to hold base salaries at a level that gives people a great deal of job security—that pretty much guarantees they'll have work so long as they do a decent job. But if they do a better-than-decent job, if they can figure out ways to improve, the company shares with them whatever additional money they generate by paying them bonuses. The more they generate, the bigger the bonuses. It's like getting a raise, maybe even a very substantial raise, over and above your regular salary, but in a way that doesn't jeopardize your future employment. We know we can survive the tough economic periods. We may not pay bonuses in tough times, but we'll keep going. We won't lose jobs.

In effect, we're creating a certain elasticity for the down times. We don't ever want to lay people off, and we don't want to cut wages, either. Most of the salary a working person earns goes to cover his or her fixed costs—mortgage, tuition, groceries, transportation expenses. If you're forced to cut back in those areas, your morale is going to tumble. I don't know of anything harder than having to cut basic living expenses. We want people to be able to count on a certain level of income, but we also want to give them the opportunity to earn more. And they will earn a lot more as long as the company is in good shape and they are performing up to their capabilities.

If Bonus Programs Are So Great, Why Do So Many of Them Fail?

Probably for a lot of reasons our bonus program failed in 1983. It was a total disaster. For one thing, most people didn't understand it. They weren't motivated by it. They didn't know what they could do to achieve the goals. Not only that, but we'd chosen the wrong goals. We wouldn't have had enough cash to cover the bonuses if people *had* hit the targets. When we realized our mistake, we killed the program immediately, midway through the year, and went back to the drawing boards. That experience taught us how *not* to set up a bonus program. We've learned a lot since then about developing one that really works. In the process, we've come up with a checklist of what you should do, and what you should avoid, when you create your own bonus plan.

Do's and Don'ts for Bonus Programs
Put Everybody in the Same Boat

Every employee should be part of the same bonus program, from the chief executive to the people who sweep the floors and answer the phones. Give everybody the same goals and a similar stake in the outcome. At SRC, we calculate bonuses as a percentage of regular compensation. Whenever a bonus is paid under Stop-Gooter, each of us gets a check for an amount representing a preset percentage of our annual pay (salary, or wages plus overtime).

We don't all get the same percentage, however. Under Stop-Gooter, most managers and professionals are eligible to earn bonuses totaling up to 18% of their annual pay. For everyone else, the maximum bonus is 13% of annual pay. The reason is simple: we want people to move ahead, to take more risks and shoulder additional responsibilities. If they do, it's important that they get rewarded. But, that said, we want everyone to go after the same goals and to be subject to the same rules.

That's because we want people to play together as a team, to pull in the same direction. It's easier to win that way. We don't want people or departments to compete against one another. We don't want to set up squads that try to beat one another. We certainly don't want to pit managers against workers, or vice versa. We want a compensation system that encourages people to understand one another's problems, that gets them to work things out. We want people to see how much we all depend on each other, regardless of where we stand in the company. At SRC, you win when everybody wins, when the company wins. I don't want a company-wide bonus program in which some people win and others lose. The only ones who lose should be our competitors.

The one exception to this rule is safety. You have to generate awareness of safety as an issue, because that's the only way to prevent accidents, and I don't have any problem doing that through internal competition. We don't include safety in our Stop-Gooter program. Instead, we run separate safety contests in which we divide the company into teams, deliberately mixing people across department lines. One year, for example, I was on a team with all the people whose last name started with S. The idea was to see which team could go the longest without an accident, and we offered $62,000 in prizes. By reducing accidents, we managed to bring down our annual workers' compensation premiums by $100,000. So the safety program wound up netting the company 38 cents on the dollar. It was a win for SRC, and a win for everyone at SRC because the savings helped us on our Stop-Gooter goals for the year.

But our main purpose was to get people thinking about safety and to keep them from getting hurt.

Stick to Two or Three Goals—and Get Them from the Financials

Giving people a long list of goals is like not having any goals at all. Build your bonus program around two or, at most, three goals per year. More than that just gets too complicated. The important thing is to choose the right ones. I want goals that keep people focused on the fundamentals of business: making money and generating cash. I also want goals that educate people about the different aspects of the business, that teach people exactly what it takes to be successful, that provide an incentive to do the right things. Finally, I want goals that make the company stronger by eliminating our weaknesses. As it turns out, you can get all of that by choosing your goals from the financial statements.

We almost always base one of our annual goals on pretax profit margins to ensure people stay focused on making money. The other goal has varied from year to year, depending on what we've seen as our biggest vulnerability at the time. As a general rule, however, we make a point of taking the second goal off the balance sheet, to make sure people also pay attention to generating cash.

Now, a funny thing happens when you choose goals from the financial statements. For every one you pick, you get about five or six others at the same time. Suppose we decide to go after liquidity, which you can measure by looking at what accountants call the current ratio. It's calculated by adding up all of your current assets (i.e., those you expect to convert to cash within the next 12 months, such as inventory and receivables) and dividing by all of your current liabilities (i.e., those you have to pay within 12 months, such as short-term debts and payables.) The ideal current ratio can vary greatly from industry to industry, but you almost always want to have more current assets than current liabilities. A ratio of two to one is generally considered quite healthy.

Whenever you can quantify a goal, you can set targets. You can decide how big a bonus people will earn by improving the current ratio a specific amount. To hit that target they have to pay attention to a whole range of factors: inventory levels, shipping schedules, operating efficiency, collection of receivables, negotiated terms with customers, and on and on. In the process, people get interested in various aspects of the business. Suddenly everybody wants to know about receivables. We have staff meetings where our accountant talks about which customers pay and how fast they pay. And people are interested because if customers don't pay, we don't have the cash—the customers do. And we can't use that cash, say, to reduce our short-term debt. And if we don't pay down the debt, we don't hit the liquidity goal, and we don't get that bonus.

So the bonus game takes people down the money trail, and they see everything that happens when customers are slow in paying their bills. They get an education in business and numbers and the accounting system. They learn how it all fits together. And they accomplish several goals in the course of going after one.

Give People the Chance to Win Early and Often

A bonus program is first and foremost a tool for motivating people. If it doesn't motivate, it isn't working. And what gets people motivated? Winning. There's really nothing like winning to make you want to go back and try again to do even better the next time. Set up your bonus program so that you put people on a winning track from the outset and then make it possible for them to keep winning right through to the end of the year.

That's the whole logic behind our system of payouts. After we choose a goal, we set the levels at which we will pay bonuses. There may be as many as five payout levels for each goal. With the profit goal, for example, the company's baseline is usually a pretax margin of 5%, while our top target is 8.6%. If we come in with a pretax profit margin below 5%, we don't earn any bonuses. If it's between 5 and 5.5%, we get into the first payout level, which pays hourly people bonuses equal to 1.3% of their regular pay. We hit the second level at a pretax margin of 5.6%, and the bonus rises to 2.6%. The third level starts at the 6.6% margin and pays 3.9% of regular pay. So it goes until the company gets to an 8.6% margin or better, at which point an hourly employee earns a maximum payout on the profit goal of 6.5%.

Coming up with the specific targets and payout levels is largely a matter of arithmetic. The numbers will, of course, be different for each company. You *must* do the math. The bonus system won't work if the math doesn't work. In making your calculations, however, do not lose sight of the fundamental purpose, namely, to get and keep your people motivated. Following are some general rules to bear in mind.

Set the baseline at the lowest point that still guarantees the company's security. Everybody must understand that the basic health of the company is paramount. Nobody should earn a bonus for doing the minimum required to protect jobs. We figure, for example, that a pretax profit margin of 5% is the lowest we can have without getting into trouble. (Remember, 40% of profits go to taxes, so that leaves us with about a 3% after-tax margin, which we need for working capital—replacing worn-out machines, handling swings in inventory, and so on.) On the other hand, you don't want to put the baseline so high that people get discouraged right off the bat. Keep the first payout level well within their range. At SRC, everybody knows we are capable of getting into the first level on either goal, because we set the baseline at a level we've already achieved in the past.

Notice that people are focusing *above* the survival point. Many companies set their goals too low, as if it's okay to break even. Then the company is in danger if people miss the goal. We never want to operate that close to the line. If our pretax margin is less than 5%, we all feel as though we've let one another down, and that's exactly how I want it. I would rather have people feel bad about missing the bonus than about losing their jobs because the company is not making money.

Make sure people have the opportunity to take home a significant portion of the additional profits generated under the bonus plan. Bonuses won't motivate people if they think the company is being cheap or greedy, or if the rewards aren't commensurate with the effort they're being asked to put out. They must feel that the plan is both a fair deal and a way to earn some big bucks. Stop-Gooter gives a machinist on the shop floor a shot at getting an extra 13% on top of his or her base compensation—that's $2,600 for someone making $20,000 a year. As for the company, it gives back to people, in the form of bonuses, about half of the additional profits generated over and above the base of 5% pretax (assuming we hit the highest payout levels on both goals).

Make it possible for people to earn bonuses frequently enough to keep them involved in the Game. One of the most common mistakes companies make is to have just one bonus payout per year. Then they compound the mistake by not announcing how much people have earned until long after the year-end, and not actually paying it for several weeks beyond that. What happens is that people ignore the bonus program until the final quarter—if you're lucky. More likely, they pay no attention to it at all and regard whatever they get under it as a gift. That kind of bonus is not a reward; it's a bribe.

We set up the Stop-Gooter program so that people have a chance to earn a bonus every three months. That makes sense because of our overall approach to "the Great Game of Business." On the one hand, we want people to get used to a quarterly grading system: it's a time-tested way of evaluating companies, and it works. It fits in with the normal cycles of a business. It's a good short-term time frame. Moreover, the three-month period turns out to be pretty much ideal for the way we play the Game. The end of the quarter comes fast enough that we can keep people focused on it through our weekly meetings.

Not every bonus program should have quarterly payouts. Monthly bonuses might work better for some companies. I can also see having semiannual ones. Don't go longer than that, however, without at least locking in the money owed to people. Not only will the bonus lose its impact, but you may run into credibility problems, especially if the program is new. People are going to be skeptical when you lay out the bonus deal for them. They won't really believe it until they see the money in their hands. But once that happens, their attitude will change so fast it will take your breath away.

Start with a small bonus pool and let it grow as the year goes on, so that people have the opportunity and the incentive to meet all the goals—and earn the entire bonus—right up to the end. By "bonus pool" I mean the total amount of money available to be paid out in bonuses during any given period. I'm saying the pool should start small and grow from month to month or quarter to quarter. This is a very important point. If you are not careful, you might inadvertently build some subtle demotivators into your plan. Suppose you decide to give people the chance to earn 25% of the annual bonus in each quarter of the year, and they come up short in the first two quarters. That would take a lot of steam out of the program. People might well get demoralized and stop trying. Suppose, on the other hand, they simply had to achieve the goals at any point in order to earn the bonus for the entire year—and they got everything done by the middle of the third quarter. Chances are that the company would be headed for big trouble before the year was through.

We avoid these pitfalls by increasing the stakes as the year goes on and by rolling any unearned bonus from one quarter into the pot for the next quarter. Here's how it works: the bonus pool for the first quarter is 10% of the total for the year. For the second quarter, it's 20%; for the third quarter, it's 30%; for the fourth quarter, it's 40%. Let's say we hit half of our targets in the first quarter and thus earn half of the available bonus. That amounts to 5% (half of 10%) of the total bonus we are eligible to earn during the year. We get paid the 5% we've earned right away; the unearned 5% is rolled over into the second quarter pool. So now, in the second quarter, we are going after 25% of the annual bonus pool (the 20% share for the second quarter, plus the 5% share left over from the first quarter). Suppose we don't hit any of our targets in the second quarter. In that case, the entire 25% gets rolled into the third quarter, which means we are now shooting for 55% of the annual bonus (the 30% share from the third quarter, plus the 20% from the second, plus the 5% from the first). Even if we hit all of our highest targets in the third quarter, there is 40% of the bonus pool available to go after in the fourth quarter. If we don't hit any of our targets, we still have a chance to earn the rest of the annual bonus (95%) before the end of the year.

As a result, people stay in the game right up to the last whistle. We can win one quarter at a time, or we can pull it out on a Hail Mary pass in the final seconds. Like the man said, it ain't over 'til the fat lady sings—and, by then, we have another game ready to go.

Communicate, Communicate, Communicate

Above all, make sure people understand how the bonus program works and are kept up-to-date on how they're doing. Bad communication is the main reason most bonus systems fail. No matter how clever you have been, no matter how well you have chosen your goals, no matter how carefully you have designed your pay-out system, your program simply won't motivate people if they don't get it, if they can't follow what's happening, or if they think you're hiding something from them. Don't expect them to give you the benefit of the doubt. I guarantee that they will think you're manipulating the numbers if there is any doubt about the bonus formula, or if you lack a system for monitoring and checking the results.

Of course, if the bonus program makes sense, explaining it shouldn't be all that difficult. Start by teaching the teachers—that is, your managers, supervisors, and key employees. Develop a solid core of people who know what's going on and who can explain it to everyone else. It's a good idea to hold some meetings and produce some support materials (handouts, brochures, videos, whatever). But once your teachers are up to speed, don't wait. Go ahead and launch the program. Most people are going to learn about the bonus game the way people have always learned about games: by playing it.

What's crucial is to have an effective system for keeping track of the results and communicating them throughout the company. Set a day and a time when the latest score will be announced each week (or, if that's not possible, each month) and then make sure you hit it. People will start looking forward to these updates. *Do not disappoint them.* If you are late with the scores, you will feed people's doubts and suspicions, dampen their enthusiasm, and undermine your chances of success.

How you communicate the results is up to you. Post them. Hold meetings. Put notices in with the paychecks. Set up an electronic ticker tape in the cafeteria and flash the score at lunch. If your people are spread out geographically, send the results out by fax or announce them by teleconference. Whatever you do, give people every opportunity to ask questions and get explanations. And go out of your way to make available the numbers on which the scores are based. Whether people actually check up on you or not, they want to know that they could if they had to. That's one reason for publishing complete, detailed financial statements every month. Ours run to a hundred pages, beginning with the monthly Stop-Gooter results. People could do their own calculations, if they were so inclined, from the numbers in the income statement and the balance sheet.

But keeping everybody up-to-date on the score is just part of the process required to make the bonus program work. In fact, the program should become the center of attention in your business. It should provide a context and a structure for everything else that goes on. If you've chosen the right goals, after all, achieving them should be everybody's top priority—by definition.

For the bonus program to play that role, there has to be a continuous, two-way flow of information between the people on the front lines and the managers who are overseeing the action. The top managers need numbers they can use to identify problems that should be solved, opportunities that should be pursued, victories that should be celebrated. The front-line people need constant updates on where they stand, and they have to be shown what they can do to improve the results. The middle managers need tools to motivate and to lead; to set priorities; and to draw the connection between meeting the standards, hitting the targets, and earning the bonus.

Obviously, we are talking about fundamental questions of management here. That's perhaps the most important benefit of a good bonus program. It provides a powerful incentive to make sure people throughout the organization have a clear understanding of their roles and the information required to perform them as well as possible. A company's ability to manage the flow of information will go a long way toward determining not only the effectiveness of its bonus program but also its ultimate success in the marketplace.

At SRC, we manage the flow of information by playing "the Great Game of Business." The principal mechanism we use is the weekly staff meeting, which is not so much a discrete event as the focal point for the entire process of exchanging information up and down the organization.

Don't Pay the Bonus Unless It Is Earned (But Do Everything You Can to Help People Win)

This is a simple point, but it is fundamental. The bonus program should be a tool for putting people in touch with the realities of the marketplace. A bonus should not be seen as a gift from management. It should be a reward people earn by doing a better job than their competitors who are out there vying for the same customers. You undermine that message if you pay the bonus when people come up short on their targets.

This can be very, very tough for a CEO. If people have tried hard and missed by a tiny amount, there is a big temptation to pay the bonus anyway. Resist it. Once you start changing the rules of the game, you step onto a slippery slope, and it is hard to go back. A couple of times, we have missed targets by .01%. In each case, it was agony. I never want it to happen again. So now, as we near the end of the quarter, our accountants come into the weekly meeting with sheets showing exactly what we must do to get to the next level on each goal. You can always come up with a few thousand dollars extra in some area, if that's what it takes.

Conclusion

The real power of the bonus program lies in its ability to educate people about business. Once they understand the math, they see how everything fits together, and how business can be a tool for getting them what they want. And it all does fit together. The system really works. You can't criticize it, because it is simply a reflection of reality. You can criticize individuals. You can take people to task for the way they do business. You can go after the ones who are greedy, who only want to help themselves, who exploit other people for personal gain. But the fault lies in those individuals, not in the nature of capitalism.

A Primer on Sharing Equity with Employees

Corey Rosen

Many companies, both publicly traded and privately held, want to provide employees with a stake in the company as an incentive or reward for their work. While giving employees cash bonuses, profit sharing, extra vacation, a company car, or other perquisites can be very valued, sharing equity is unique in its ability to link the employee's interests to the long-term growth of company value. Because equity plans can so easily be designed to require employees to earn their shares through future years of service or meeting certain performance targets, they also can be ideal mechanisms for getting employees to focus on long-term goals—and to stay around long enough to make sure those goals are met.

Equity can be shared in a variety of ways. Some plans, such as employee stock ownership plans (ESOPs) and 401(k) plans invested in company stock, are benefit plans that must follow rules of the Employee Retirement Income Security Act (ERISA) concerning who gets how much, when they get it, and what rights they have. Other plans, such as employee stock purchase plans (ESPPs), must be offered to all employees meeting minimum requirements, but the employee must make the choice to invest in stock, often at a discount and with an opportunity to buy the stock at a price set 3 to 24 months earlier. These plans can be and are used as employee rewards and incentives, but they are not (and cannot be) designed to provide specific employees with specifically tailored incentives.

Individual equity plans, including stock options, restricted stock and restricted stock units, phantom stock, and stock appreciation rights can be given to any employee under any set of criteria. In return for this flexibility, these plans do not carry significant tax benefits, with the exception of incentive stock options (ISOs). The employee's gains from ISOs can be taxed as capital gains, but the company then gives up any tax deduction.

This chapter is not a substitute for detailed investigation of the particular plans chosen. All of these plans involve often complex tax, accounting, planning, administration, financing, and feasibility issues. Instead, this chapter provides a very basic overview to help decision-makers understand the array of choices available.

The first part of the chapter looks at individual equity plans; these plans can be used for either selective or broad-based equity sharing. The second part looks at plans that are designed to benefit most or all employees. The chapter focuses on plan design and tax issues. Securities law considerations are briefly discussed, but because this is such a complex subject, they are not reviewed in any detail. Accounting issues are extremely complex and varied for different plans and are discussed only very briefly here. For more information on accounting concerns, see the NCEO's *Accounting for Equity Compensation* (for individual equity plans and ESPPs) or *Leveraged ESOPs and Employee Buyouts* (for ESOPs).

Basic Forms of Individual Equity Plans

There are four basic kinds of individual equity compensation plans: stock options, restricted stock and restricted stock units, stock appreciation rights, and phantom stock. Some of these plans have variations as well. Each plan provides employees with some special consideration in price or terms. We do not cover here simply offering employees the right to buy stock as any other investor would.

Stock options give employees the right to buy a number of shares at a price fixed at grant for a defined number of years into the future. *Restricted stock* (and its close relative *restricted stock units*) give employees the right to acquire or receive shares, by gift or purchase, once certain restrictions, such as working a certain number of years or meeting a performance target, are met. *Phantom stock* pays a future cash bonus equal to the value of a certain number of shares. *Stock appreciation rights* (SARs) provide the right to the increase in the value of a designated number of shares, usually paid in cash, but occasionally settled in shares (this is called a "stock-settled SAR").

Stock Options

A few key concepts help define how stock options work:

Exercise: The purchase of stock with an option.

Exercise price: The price at which the stock can be purchased. This is also called the *strike price* or *grant price*. In most plans, the exercise price is the current fair market value of the stock at the time the grant is made.

Spread: The difference between the exercise price and the market value of the stock at the time of exercise.

Option term: The length of time the employee can hold the option before it expires.

Vesting: The process by which the right to exercise options is earned, usually by years of service.

A company grants an employee options to buy a stated number of shares at a defined grant price. The options vest over a period of time or once certain individual, group, or corporate goals are met. Once vested, the employee can exercise the option at the grant price at any time over the option term up to the expiration date. For instance, an employee might be granted the right to buy 1,000 shares at $10 per share. The options vest 25% per year over four years and have a term of 10 years. If the stock goes up, the employee will pay $10 per share to buy the stock. The difference between the $10 grant price and the exercise price is the spread. If the stock goes to $25 after seven years, and the employee exercises all options, the spread would be $15 per share.

Kinds of Options

Option plans are either incentive stock options (ISOs) or nonqualified options (NSOs). When an employee exercises a nonqualified stock option, the spread on exercise is taxable to the employee as ordinary income, even if the shares are not yet sold. A corresponding amount is deductible by the company. There is no legally required holding period for the shares after exercise, although the company may impose one. Any subsequent gain or loss on the shares after exercise is taxed as a capital gain or loss.

An incentive stock option (ISO) enables an employee to (1) defer taxation on the option from the date of exercise until the date of sale of the underlying shares, and (2) pay tax at capital gains rates, rather than ordinary income tax rates, on the spread at exercise. Certain conditions must be met to qualify for ISO treatment:

1. The employee must hold the stock for at least one year after the exercise date or two years after the grant date, whichever is later.

2. Only $100,000 of stock options can first become exercisable in any year. This is measured by the grant price of the options, not the exercise price. It means that only $100,000 in grant price value can vest (first become exercisable) in any one year. If there is overlapping vesting, such as would occur if options are granted annually and vest gradually, companies must track outstanding options to see whether the amount that becomes vested under different grants will exceed $100,000 in grant value in any one year.

3. The exercise price must not be less than the market price of the company's stock on the date of the grant.

4. Only employees can qualify for ISOs.

5. The option must be granted pursuant to a written plan that has been approved by shareholders and that specifies how many

shares can be issued under the plan and identifies the class of employees eligible to receive the options. Options must be granted within 10 years of the date of the adoption of the plan.

6. The option must be exercised within 10 years of the date of the grant.

7. The employee cannot own, at the time of the grant, more than 10% of the voting power of all outstanding stock of the company, unless the exercise price is at least 110% of the market value of the stock on the date of the grant and the option is not exercisable more than five years from the date of the grant.

8. ISOs can only be issued to employees.

If all the rules for incentive options are met at the time of exercise, then the transaction is called a "qualifying disposition," and the employee pays capital gains tax on the total increase in value at sale over the grant price. However, the spread on the option at exercise is a "preference item" for purposes of the alternative minimum tax (AMT). So even though the shares may not have been sold, the exercise requires the employee to add back the gain on exercise, along with other AMT preference items, to see whether an alternative minimum tax payment is due.

The company does not take a tax deduction when there is a qualifying disposition. If, however, there is a disqualifying disposition, most often because the employee exercises and sells before meeting the required holding periods, the spread on exercise is taxable to the employee at ordinary income tax rates, and any capital appreciation on the ISO shares in excess of the market price on exercise is taxed at capital gains rates. In this instance, the company may then deduct the spread on exercise.

The second kind of option is a nonqualified option (NSO). NSOs can be issued to anyone—employees, directors, consultants, suppliers, customers, etc. There are no special tax benefits for NSOs, however. Like an ISO, there is no tax on the grant of the option, but when it is exercised, the spread between the grant and exercise price is taxable as ordinary income. The company receives a corresponding tax deduction. If the employee holds the stock after exercise, any subsequent appreciation in value will result in capital gains tax as of the time of sale.

Exercising an Option

There are four ways to exercise a stock option: cash, the exchange of existing shares (often called a stock swap), same-day sales, and their close relative, sell-to-cover sales (these latter two are often called cashless exercises, although that term actually includes other exercise methods described here as well). Any one company, however, may provide for just one or two of these alternatives. Private companies do not offer same-day or sell-to-cover sales, and, not infrequently, restrict the exercise or sale of the shares acquired through exercise until the company is sold or goes public.

The most common form of exercise for an option in a closely held company is simply for the employee to pay cash for the shares. The employee might then have additional taxes due, depending on the kind of option. If the options are nonqualified, the employer might then have to withhold taxes on the spread from the employee's future paychecks, unless the employer can arrange to use some of the option shares to pay for this obligation, as would normally be the case in the kind of cashless transactions described below.

In a same-day sale, the employee works with a broker, usually one provided by the company. The company provides the broker with enough shares to cover the option exercise, the broker turns around and sells them, and the proceeds, minus the exercise price and any taxes due, go to the employee. Although called a "same-day" sale, the process can take up to three days. In a sell-to-cover exercise, the same approach is used, but the broker sells only enough shares to cover the exercise price and any taxes due, giving the employee the remaining value in shares.

In a stock swap, the employee simply exchanges existing shares for the option shares. For instance, if the employee has the right to buy 1,000 shares at $10 per share, and the shares are now worth $25, the employee would exchange 400 shares the employee currently owns for the 1,000 shares. That's because the 400 shares the employee owns are worth $10,000. The employee would then get

600 shares from the option. If there are taxes due as well, then the employee might choose to turn in enough shares to cover the taxes as well, although this would not be a common strategy. Stock swaps are more commonly used with incentive stock options where taxes do not have to be paid until the newly acquired shares are sold.

Accounting

Under the new accounting standard for equity compensation plans, Statement of Financial Accounting Standards 123 (revised 2004) ("FAS 123(R)"), companies must calculate the present value of all option awards as of the date of grant and show this as a charge to compensation. The value should be adjusted based on vesting experience (so unvested shares do not count as a charge to compensation).

Publicly traded companies must adopt FAS 123(R) by their first interim or annual fiscal period beginning after June 15, 2005 (December 15, 2005, for small business issuers). The new standard applies to any options and other equity awards granted after adoption of the standard and any options or awards granted before adoption that are not yet vested. Privately held companies must adopt the standard by their first annual fiscal period beginning after December 15, 2005. For privately held companies that used a minimum value model to account for stock options under FAS No. 123, the new standard applies only to options and awards granted after adoption; it does not apply to any options or awards granted prior to adoption. In addition, these companies are not permitted to voluntarily restate prior fiscal periods.

Deferred Compensation Rules

Employees could always defer the receipt of a vested (and thus taxable) equity award under deferred compensation plans by making an election. Rules for how to do this were ambiguous in the past. Under new Internal Revenue Code Section 409A, added by the American Jobs Creation Act of 2004, employees will be able to elect to defer only if several conditions are met:

1. The employee dies, becomes disabled, there is a change in control, there is an unforeseen emergency (as rigorously defined in the law), or there is a fixed date or schedule specified by the plan.

2. Elections for deferral must be made not later than the close of the preceding taxable year in which the award would vest or, if made in the first year of the award, within 30 days after the employee first becomes eligible for an award. If the employee is a key employee (as defined by statute) of a public company, receipt of the benefit must be not earlier than six months after separation

3. If the award is performance-based, the election must come not later than six months before the end of the performance period.

4. There can be no acceleration of benefits once a deferral election has been made.

5. Any subsequent elections for an award must be at least twelve months after the prior election and must defer receipt for at least five years in the future.

The new deferred compensation rules do not apply to qualified benefit plans, such as ESOPs or 401(k) plans, as well as sick leave, death benefits, and similar arrangements. Incentive stock options are also not covered by the new rules, and nonqualified options are not covered unless they are issued at less than fair market value. The effective date is December 31, 2004, but deferrals made after October 2, 2004, under a plan that has been materially modified after that date are covered. Tax-qualified ESPPs under Section 423 of the Internal Revenue Code are not covered.

Valuation

Under the new deferred compensation rules, to determine whether a nonqualified option is issued at fair market value in a closely held company, a company must establish a mechanism to know what fair market value is. Similarly, under regulations issued in 2004 for incentive stock options, to meet the "$100,000 rule," closely held companies also have to establish a fair market value. Unfortunately, there is no specific guidance on just what the IRS would allow as an acceptable valuation technique. There is a safe harbor method of using two independent appraisals contemporaneous with the issuance of each award, but few closely held companies will want to do that. Most advisors believe that a single independent appraisal would probably suffice, or even a rigorous process established by the board, but there is no certainty about this.

Restricted Stock

Restricted stock plans provide employees with the right to purchase shares at fair market value or a discount, or it simply grants shares to employees outright. However, the shares employees acquire are not really theirs yet—they cannot take possession of the shares until specified restrictions lapse. Most commonly, the restriction is that the employee work for the company for a certain number of years, often three to five. The time-based restrictions may pass all at once or gradually. Any restrictions could be imposed, however. The company could, for instance, restrict the shares until certain corporate, departmental, or individual performance goals are achieved. With restricted stock units (RSUs), employees do not actually buy or receive shares *until* the restrictions lapse. In effect, RSUs are like phantom stock settled in shares instead of cash.

While the shares are subject to restrictions, companies can choose whether to pay dividends, provide voting rights, or give the employee other benefits of being a shareholder. When employees are awarded the restricted stock, they have the right to make what is called a "Section 83(b)" election, much as they can make this election for a stock option. If they make the election, they are taxed at ordinary income tax rates on the "bargain element" of the award at the time of grant. If the shares are simply granted to the employee, then the bargain element is their full value. If some consideration is paid, then the tax is based on the difference between what is paid and the fair market value at the time of the grant. If full price is paid, there is no tax. Any future increase in the value of the shares until they are sold is then taxed as capital gains, not ordinary income. If employees do not make the election, then there is no tax until the restrictions lapse, at which time ordinary income tax is due on the difference between the grant and exercise price. Subsequent changes in value are capital gains (or losses). RSUs do not allow employees to make the Section 83(b) election.

The employer gets a tax deduction only for amounts employees pay income tax on, regardless of whether a Section 83(b) election is made or not. A Section 83(b) election carries some risk. If the employee makes the election and pays tax, but the restrictions never lapse, the employee does not get the taxes paid refunded, nor does the employee get the shares.

Restricted stock accounting parallels option accounting in most respects. If the only restriction is vesting, companies account for restricted stock by first determining the total compensation cost at the time the award is made. So if the employee is simply given 1,000 restricted shares worth $10 per share, then a $10,000 cost is incurred. If the employee buys the shares at fair value, no charge is recorded; if there is a discount, that counts as a cost. The cost is then amortized over the period of vesting until the restrictions lapse. Because the accounting is based on the initial cost, companies with a low share price will find that a vesting requirement for the award means their accounting charge will be very low even if the stock price goes up.

If the award is more contingent, such as performance vesting, the value must be adjusted each year for the current stock price, then amortized over the estimated life of the award (the time estimated to meet the performance goal). Each year, the expected cost is amortized over the estimated remaining expected life. So if the stock is awarded at $10 and goes to $15 in the first year of an expected five-year term, then $15 × 1,000 × .20 is recorded ($3,000). If the price goes to $18 the next year, the calculation is $18 × 1,000 × .40 ($7,200). The prior $3,000 is subtracted from this amount, yielding a charge of $4,200 for that year.

Restricted stock is not subject to the new deferred compensation plan rules, but restricted stock units are.

Phantom Stock and Stock Appreciation Rights

Stock appreciation rights (SARs) and phantom stock are very similar plans. Both essentially are cash bonus plans, although some plans pay out the benefits in the form of shares. SARs typically provide the employee with a cash payment based on the increase in the value of a stated number of shares over a specific period of time. Phantom stock provides a cash or stock bonus based on the value of a stated number of shares, to be paid out at the end of a specified period of time. SARs may not have a specific settlement date; like options, the employees may have flexibility in when to choose to exercise the SAR. Phantom stock may pay dividends; SARs would not. When the payout is made, it is taxed as ordinary income to the employee and is deductible to the employer. Some phantom plans condition the receipt of the award on meeting certain objectives, such as sales, profits, or other targets. These plans often refer to their phantom stock as "performance units." Phantom stock and SARs can be given to anyone, but if they are given out broadly to employees, there is a possibility that they will be considered retirement plans and will be subject to federal retirement plan rules. Careful plan structuring can avoid this problem.

Because SARs and phantom plans are essentially cash bonuses or are delivered in the form of stock that holders will want to cash in, companies need to figure out how to pay for them. Does the company just make a promise to pay, or does it really put aside the funds? If the award is paid in stock, is there a market for the stock? If it is only a promise, will employees believe the benefit is as phantom as the stock? If it is in real funds set aside for this purpose, the company will be putting after-tax dollars aside and not in the business. Many small, growth-oriented companies cannot afford to do this. The fund can also be subject to excess accumulated earnings tax. On the other hand, if employees are given shares, the shares can be paid for by capital markets if the company goes public or by acquirers if the company is sold.

If phantom stock or SARs are irrevocably promised to employees, it is possible the benefit will become taxable before employees actually receive the funds. A "rabbi trust," a segregated account to fund deferred payments to employees, may help solve the accumulated earnings problem, but if the company is unable to pay creditors with existing funds, the money in these trusts goes to them. Telling employees their right to the benefit is not irrevocable or is dependent on some condition (working another five years, for instance) may prevent the money from being currently taxable, but it may also weaken employee belief that the benefit is real.

Finally, if phantom stock or SARs are intended to benefit most or all employees and defer some or all payment until termination or later, they may be considered de facto "ERISA plans." ERISA (the Employee Retirement Income Security Act of 1974) is the federal law that governs retirement plans. It does not allow non-ERISA plans to operate like ERISA plans, so the plan could be ruled subject to all the constraints of ERISA. Similarly, if there is an explicit or implied reduction in compensation to get the phantom stock, there could be securities issues involved, most likely anti-fraud disclosure requirements. Plans designed just for a limited number of employees, or as a bonus for a broader group of employees that pays out annually based on a measure of equity, would most likely avoid these problems. Moreover, the regulatory issues are gray areas; it could be that a company could use a broad-based plan that pays over longer periods or at departure and not ever be challenged.

Phantom stock and SAR accounting is straightforward. When the awards are settled in cash, these plans are treated in the same way as deferred cash compensation. As the amount of the liability changes each year, an entry is made for the amount accrued. A decline in value would create a negative entry. These entries are not contingent on vesting. In closely held companies, share value is often stated as book value. However, this can dramatically underrate the true value of a company, especially one based primarily on intellectual capital. Having an outside appraisal performed, therefore, can make the plans much more accurate rewards for employee contributions.

If phantom stock or SAR awards are settled in stock, the accounting is more similar to stock option accounting. A present value estimate of the award cost must be made at grant, and it can be adjusted later to correct for forfeitures.

Phantom stock and SARs settled in cash, as well as grants of SARs settled in stock in closely held companies, are also now subject to deferred compensation rules under Section 409A of the Internal Revenue Code. If an employee desires to defer the receipt of such an award to a future taxable year, these rules require the employee to make an election to defer receipt within 30 days after the grant of the award and at least 12 months before the end of the vesting period. If an award vests in June 2010, for example, and the employee desires to receive his or her payout in June 2011, the election would have to be made within 30 days of the grant and no later than June 2009.

Stock appreciation rights are not subject to the new deferred compensation rules if they are settled in stock of public companies. Cash-settled SARs and phantom stock are subject to the new rules. SARs in public companies only qualify, however, if:

- The exercise price is never less than the fair market value at grant.
- There is no additional deferral provision.
- The SAR is not part of a tandem arrangement with a stock option under which the SAR is paid in cash; in that case, the option will be considered deferred compensation.

SARs granted before October 3, 2004, are excluded for closely held companies as well if they meet the last three rules.

Employee Stock Purchase Plans

Millions of employees become owners in their companies through employee stock purchase plans (ESPPs). Many if not most of these plans are organized under Section 423 of the Internal Revenue Code and thus are often called "Section 423" plans. Other ESPPs are "nonqualified" plans, meaning they do not have to meet the special rules of Section 423 and do not get any of the special tax treatment.

Under Section 423, companies must allow all employees to participate, but they can exclude those with less than two years' tenure, part-time employees, and highly compensated employees. All employees must have the same rights and privileges under the plan, although companies can allow purchase limits to vary with relative compensation (most do not do this, however). Plans can limit how much employees can buy, and the law limits it to $25,000 per year.

Section 423 plans operate by allowing employees to have deductions taken out of their pay on an after-tax basis. These deductions accumulate over an "offering period." At a specified time or times employees can choose to use these accumulated deductions to purchase shares or they can get the money back. Plans can offer discounts of up to 15% on the price of the stock. Most plans allow this discount to be taken based on *either* the price at the beginning or end of the offering period (the so-called "look-back feature"). The offering period can last up to five years if the price employees pay for their stock is based on the share price at the end of the period or 27 months if it can be determined at an earlier point.

Plan design can vary in a number of ways. For instance, a company might allow employees a 15% discount on the price at the end of the offering period, but no discount if they buy shares based on the price at the beginning of the period. Some companies offer employees interim opportunities to buy shares during the offering period. Others provide smaller discounts. Offering periods also vary in length. NCEO studies, however, show that the large majority of plans have a look-back feature and provide 15% discounts off the share price at the beginning or end of the offering period. Most of the plans have a 12-month offering period, with six months the next most common.

The tax treatment of a Section 423 plan is similar to that of an incentive stock option except that there is an ordinary income element (unless the shares are sold at a loss), even with a qualifying disposition. If employees hold the shares for two years after grant and one year after exercise, they will realize ordinary income on the lesser of (1) the purchase price discount as of the beginning of the offering period (i.e., the market value at that time minus the purchase price) and (2) the sale price minus the purchase price. All additional gain is a long-term capital gain. If the sale price is less than the purchase price, there is a long-term capital loss for the difference between those two prices. The company receives no tax deduction. Currently, there is no withholding requirement on the gain on the employee purchase of shares; the IRS previously indicated it wanted to require withholding for FICA, FUTA, and Medicare, but at this writing, that is indefinitely on hold.

If the holding period rules are not met, there is a disqualifying disposition, and the employee recognizes ordinary income on the difference between the market price on the purchase date and the purchase price. The difference, if any, between the market price on the purchase date and the sale price is a capital gain or loss, which is long-term if the stock is held for more than one year. The company receives a deduction for the amount recognized as ordinary income.

Nonqualified ESPPs usually work much the same way as Section 423 plans, but there are no rules for how they must be structured and no special tax benefits. The employee recognizes ordinary income at the time of purchase on the difference between the market price at that time and the purchase price. The difference, if any, between the market price on the purchase date and the sale price is a capital gain or loss, which is long-term if the stock is held for more than one year. The company receives a deduction for the amount recognized as ordinary income.

ESPPs are found almost exclusively in public companies because the offering of stock to employees requires compliance with costly and complex securities laws. Closely held companies can, and sometimes do, have these plans, however. Offerings of stock only to employees can qualify for an exemption from securities registration requirements at the federal level, although they will have to comply with anti-fraud disclosure rules and, possibly, state securities laws as well. If they do offer stock in a stock purchase plan, it is highly advisable they obtain at least an annual appraisal.

ESPPs are very popular in public companies and some pre-IPO companies (where the plan starts before the IPO, and purchases are not made until after it) because they offer a benefit to employees and additional capital to companies. Any dilution resulting from the issuance of new shares to satisfy the purchase requests, or from the company repurchasing outstanding shares and reselling them at a discount, is usually so small that shareholders do not object. Rates of participation vary widely, with the median levels around 30% to 40% of eligible employees. Because most employees do not commit large amounts to these plans, and many do not participate at all, ESPPs should generally be seen as an adjunct to other employee ownership plans, not a means in themselves to create an ownership culture.

Under the new accounting rules to be effective in 2005 or 2006, depending a company's fiscal year, ESPPs must be accounted for in the same way as options. Any discount offered counts as a compensation charge, and the present value of the option element must be calculated as an additional charge to income. However, no accounting charge is required if the discount is 5% or less and there is no look-back feature in the plan.

Section 423 ESPPs are not subject to the new deferred compensation plan rules.

Employee Stock Ownership Plans

An employee stock ownership plan (ESOP) is a kind of employee benefit plan under ERISA. ESOPs were given a specific statutory framework in 1974. Like other tax-qualified deferred compensation plans, they must not discriminate in their operations in favor of highly compensated employees, officers, or owners. In an ESOP, a company sets up an employee benefit trust, which it funds by contributing cash to buy company stock, contributing shares directly, or having the trust borrow money to buy stock, with the company making contributions to the plan to enable it to repay the loan. Generally, at least all full-time employees with a year or more of service are in the plan. Employees almost never contribute to the plan; instead, contributions are funded by the company as a benefit and allocated to employee accounts on a nondiscriminatory basis, much as in a profit sharing plan. To assure that these rules are met, ESOPs must appoint a trustee to act as the plan fiduciary. This can be anyone, although larger companies tend to appoint an outside trust institution, while smaller companies typically appoint a manager or create an ESOP trust committee. ESOPs are designed to invest primarily in the stock of the employer, and can buy shares for exiting owners, treasury shares, or newly issued shares. An ESOP can be used for many purposes, including the following:

- The most common application for an ESOP is *to buy the shares of a departing owner of a closely held company.* In C corporations, owners can defer tax on the gain they have made from the sale to an ESOP if the ESOP holds more than 30% of the company's stock (and certain other requirements are met). Moreover, the purchase can be made in pretax corporate dollars.

- ESOPs are also used *to divest or acquire subsidiaries, buy back shares from the market (including public companies seeking a takeover defense), or restructure existing benefit plans* by replacing current benefit contributions with a leveraged ESOP.

- Companies can use an ESOP *to buy newly issued shares in the company, with the borrowed funds being used to buy new productive capital.* The company can, in effect, finance growth or acquisitions in pretax dollars while these same dollars create an employee benefit plan.

- Finally, an ESOP can simply be *an employee benefit plan* for companies that want to share ownership broadly. In public companies especially, an ESOP contribution is often used as part or all of a match to employee deferrals to an 401(k) plan.

Funding

The most sophisticated use of an ESOP is to borrow money (a "leveraged" ESOP). The company borrows money from a lender and reloans it to the ESOP; the ESOP uses the money to buy shares. The company makes tax-deductible contributions to the trust to enable it to repay the loan. The company can also use dividends on the shares to repay the loan; these dividends become deductible to the company. In effect, the parallel loan structure allows the company to borrow money to acquire stock and, by funneling the loan through the ESOP, deduct both principal and interest. The company can use proceeds from the loan for any legitimate business purpose. Sellers to an ESOP can also be lenders. The stock is put into a "suspense account," where it is released to employee accounts as the loan is repaid.

The ESOP can also be funded directly by discretionary corporate contributions of cash to buy existing shares or simply by the contribution of shares. These contributions are tax-deductible, generally up to 25% of the pay of the total payroll of plan participants.

How Shares Get to Employees

The rules for ESOPs are similar to the rules for other tax-qualified plans in terms of participation, allocation, vesting, and distribution, but several special considerations apply. All employees over age 21 who work for more than 1,000 hours in a plan year must be included in the plan unless they are covered by a collective bargaining unit (and the ESOP issue is negotiated in good faith), are in a separate line of business with at least 50 employees not covered by the ESOP, or fall into one of several limited anti-discrimination exemptions.

Shares are allocated to individual employee accounts based on relative compensation (generally, all W-2 compensation is counted), on a more level formula (such as per capita or seniority), or some combination. The allocated shares are subject to vesting. Employees must be 100% vested after five years of service (cliff vesting), or the company can use a graduated vesting schedule not slower than 20% after three years and 20% per year more until 100% is reached after seven years. A faster vesting schedule applies where the ESOP contribution is used as a match to employee 401(k) deferrals.

When employees reach age 55 and have 10 years of participation in the plan, the company must either give them the option of diversifying 25% of their account balances among at least three other investment alternatives, or simply pay the amount out to the employees. At age 60 with 10 years of service, employees can have 50% diversified or distributed to them.

When employees retire, die, or are disabled, the company must distribute their vested shares to them not later than the last day of the plan year following the year of their departure. For employees leaving before reaching retirement age, distribution must begin not later than the last day of the sixth plan year following their year of separation from service. Payments can be in substantially equal installments out of the trust over five years, or they can be made in a lump sum. With the installment method, a company normally pays out a portion of the stock from the trust each year.

Closely held companies and some thinly traded public companies must repurchase the shares from departing employees at their fair market value, as determined by an independent appraiser. This so-called "put option" can be exercised by the employee in one of two 60-day periods, one starting when the employee receives the distribution and the second period one year after that. The employee can choose which one to use. This obligation should be considered at the outset of the ESOP and factored into the company's ability to repay the loan.

Rules and Limitations

Shares in the plan are held in individual employee accounts. As contributions are made, they are allocated to each participant in the plan. If there is an ESOP loan, as the loan is repaid, these shares are released to the accounts of plan participants, based either on the principal paid or the percentage of total principal plus interest due that is paid that year. The amount *contributed* to repay the principal on the loan is what counts for determining if the company is within the limits for contributions allowed each year and for the purpose of calculating the tax deduction. The value of the shares released, however, is the amount used on the income statement, where it counts as a compensation cost.

Limitations on Contributions

Congress was generous in providing tax benefits for ESOPs, but there are limits. Generally, companies can contribute and deduct up to 25% of the total eligible payroll of plan participants, whether contributed in the form of cash or stock or as a payment to cover the principal portion of an ESOP loan. Interest payments on a loan are deductible as interest. Eligible pay is essentially all the pay (including employee deferrals into benefit plans) of people actually in the plan of up to $220,000 per participant (as of 2006; this and other dollar limits described here for defined contribution plans are indexed annually for inflation).

In C corporations, there are separate 25% limits for (1) contributions to pay principal on an ESOP loan and (2) contributions to other defined contribution plans; thus, a company with a leveraged ESOP and a profit sharing plan, for example, has a 50% total limit (up to 25% for a leveraged ESOP plus up to 25% for other defined contribution plans such as the profit sharing plan). However, in S corporations, company contributions to both leveraged ESOPs and other defined contribution plans all fall under a single 25% of pay calculation.

In C corporations, "reasonable" dividends paid on shares acquired by the ESOP can be used to repay an ESOP loan, and these are not included in the 25% of pay calculations. In S corporations, interest payments do count toward the applicable limits. In a leveraged ESOP, if employees leave the company before they have a fully vested right to their shares, their forfeitures, which are allocated to everyone else, are not counted in the percentage limitations.

There are a number of limitations to these provisions, however. First, no one ESOP participant can get a contribution of more than 100% of pay in any year from the principal payments on the loan or the direct ESOP contributions made that year that are attributable to that employee, or more than $44,000 (as of 2006), whichever is less. In figuring payroll, pay over $220,000 per year (as of 2006) does not count toward total contribution limits. Second, if there are other qualified benefit plans, these must be taken into account when assessing this limit. This means that employee deferrals into 401(k) plans, as well as other employer contributions to 401(k) plans, stock bonus, or profit sharing plans, are added to the ESOP contribution and cannot exceed 100% of pay or $44,000 (as of 2006) in any year.

Third, the interest on an ESOP loan repayment in a C corporation is excludable from the 25% of pay individual limit only if not more than one-third of the benefits are allocated to highly compensated employees, as defined by Internal Revenue Code Section 414(q). If the one-third rule is not met, forfeitures are also counted in determining how much an employee is getting each year.

Voting

In private companies, employees must be able to direct the trustee as to the voting of shares *allocated* to their accounts on several key issues, including closing, sale, liquidation, recapitalization, and other issues having to do with the basic structure of the company. They do not, however, have to be able to vote for the board of directors or other typical corporate governance issues, although companies can voluntarily provide these rights. Instead, the plan trustee votes the shares, usually at the direction of management. In public companies, employees must be able to vote on all issues.

What these rules mean is that for almost all ESOP companies, governance is not really an issue unless they want it to be. If companies want employees to have only the most limited role in corporate governance, they can; if they want to go beyond this, they can as well. In practice, companies that do provide employees with a substantial governance role find that it does not result in dramatic changes in the way the company is run.

Finally, in private companies and some thinly traded public companies, all ESOP transactions must be based on a current appraisal by an independent, outside valuation expert.

Tax Benefits to the Selling Shareholder

One of the major benefits of an ESOP for closely held companies is Section 1042 of the Internal Revenue Code. Under it, a seller to an ESOP may be able to qualify for a deferral of taxation of the gain made from the sale. Several requirements apply, the most significant of which are:

1. The seller must have held the stock for three years before the sale.

2. The stock must not have been acquired through stock options or other employee benefit plans.

3. The ESOP must own 30% or more of the value of the shares in the company and must continue to hold this amount for three years unless the company is sold. Shares repurchased by the company from departing employees do not count. Stock sold in a transaction that brings the ESOP to 30% of the total shares qualifies for the deferral treatment.

4. Shares qualifying for the deferral cannot be allocated to accounts of children, brothers or sisters, spouses, or parents of the selling shareholder(s), nor to any more-than-25% shareholders.

5. The company must be a "C" corporation.

If these rules are met, the seller (or sellers) can take the proceeds from the sale and reinvest them in "qualified replacement securities" within 12 months after the sale or 3 months before and defer any capital gains tax until these new investments are sold. Qualifying replacement securities are defined essentially as stocks, bonds, warrants, or debentures of domestic corporations receiving not more than 25% of their income from passive investment. Mutual funds and real estate trusts do not qualify. If the replacement securities are held until death, they are subject to a step-up in basis at that time, so capital gains taxes would never be paid.

Increasingly, lenders are asking for replacement securities as part or all of the collateral for an ESOP loan. This strategy may be beneficial to sellers selling only part of their holdings because it frees the corporation to use its assets for other borrowing and could enhance the future value of the company.

It is also important to note that people taking advantage of Section 1042 treatment cannot have stock from these sales allocated to their ESOP accounts if they remain employees. Other more-than-25% shareholders and close relatives of the seller also cannot receive allocations from these sales.

Corporate Tax Benefits

As noted, companies can use ESOPs to borrow money and repay the loan entirely in pretax dollars. In addition, companies can take a tax deduction for reasonable dividends that are used to repay a loan, that are passed through directly to employees, or that employees voluntarily reinvest in company stock. Contributions not used to pay an ESOP loan are tax-deductible as well, even if made in the form of treasury or new shares.

ESOPs in S Corporations

ESOPs can now own stock in S corporations. While these ESOPs operate under most of the same rules as they do in C corporations, there are important differences. As noted above, interest payments on ESOP loans count toward the contribution limits (they normally do not in C companies). Dividends (i.e., S corporation "distributions") paid on ESOP shares are also not deductible. Most important, sellers to an ESOP in an S corporation do not qualify for the tax-deferred Section 1042 rollover treatment.

On the other hand, the ESOP is unique among S corporation owners in that it does not have to pay federal income tax on any profits attributable to it (state rules will vary). This can make an ESOP very attractive in some cases. It also makes converting to an S corporation very appealing when a C corporation ESOP owns a high percentage of the company's stock.

For owners who want to use an ESOP to provide a market for their shares, generally it will make sense to convert to C status before setting up an ESOP. Where selling shares is not a priority, or where the seller either does not have substantial capital gains taxes due on the sale or has other reasons to prefer staying an S corporation, an S corporation ESOP can provide significant tax benefits. However, owners must keep in mind that any distributions paid to owners must be paid pro-rata to the ESOP. The ESOP can use these distributions to purchase additional shares, to build up cash for future repurchases of employee shares, or just to add to employee accounts.

While the S corporation rules make an ESOP very attractive, legislation passed in 2001 makes it clear that these rules are not meant to be abused by companies seeking to create the ESOP primarily to benefit a few people. For instance, some accountants were promoting plans in which a company would set up an S corporation management company owned by just a few people that would manage a large C corporation. The profits would flow through the S corporation, which would then not be taxed.

The rules Congress enacted are complicated, but they boil down to two essential points. First, people who own more than 10% of the allocated shares in the ESOP, or who own 20% counting their family members, are considered "disqualified" persons. The ESOP ownership is defined to include synthetic equity as well, such as options, phantom stock, and most kinds of deferred compensation. Second, if these disqualified people together own 50% or more of the company's shares (counting their synthetic equity), then they cannot get allocations in the ESOP without extraordinary tax penalties. In fact, just the accrual of an individual or family ownership interest in the plan in violation of the maximum ownership rules will trigger a penalty tax. Congress also directed the IRS to apply this onerous tax treatment to any plan it deems to be substantially for the purpose of evading taxes rather than providing employee benefits.

Financial Issues for Employees

When an employee receives a distribution from the plan, it is taxable unless rolled over into an IRA or other qualified plan. Otherwise, the amounts contributed by the employer are taxable as ordinary income, while any appreciation on the shares is taxable as capital gains. In addition, if the employee receives the distribution before normal retirement age and does not roll over the funds, a 10% excise tax is added.

While the stock is in the plan, however, it is not taxable to employees. It is rare, moreover, for employees to give up wages to participate in an ESOP or to purchase stock directly through a plan (this raises difficult securities law issues for closely held firms). Most ESOPs either are in addition to existing benefit plans or replace other defined contribution plans, usually at a higher contribution level.

Accounting

In nonleveraged plans, the contribution to the ESOP shows up directly as a compensation cost. In leveraged plans, the principal payments and dividends paid on unallocated shares to repay a loan show up as a compensation charge as well; dividends on allocated shares show up as a charge to retained earnings. The debt of the ESOP shows up as corporate debt, with an offsetting contra equity account that is reduced as the loan is repaid.

401(k) Plans

Company stock is a common component of 401(k) plans in public companies and, occasionally, closely held companies. There are several factors that favor the use of a 401(k) plan as a vehicle for employee ownership in public companies. From the company's perspective, its own stock may be one of the most cost-effective means of matching employee contributions. If there are existing treasury shares or the company prints new shares, contributing them to the 401(k) plan may impose no immediate cash cost on the company; in fact, it would provide a tax deduction. Other shareholders would suffer a dilution, of course. If the company has to buy shares to fund the match, at least the dollars being used are used to invest in itself rather than other investments. From the employee standpoint, company stock is the investment the employee knows best and so may be attractive to people who either do not want to spend the time to learn about alternatives or have a strong belief in their own company. Balanced against these advantages, of course, must be an appreciation on both the part of the employee and the company that a failure to diversify a retirement portfolio is very risky.

For closely held companies, 401(k) plans are less appealing, although they are very appropriate in some cases. If employees are given an option to buy company stock, this can often trigger securities law issues most private firms want to avoid. Employer matches make more sense, but they require the company to either dilute ownership or reacquire shares from selling shareholders. In many closely held businesses, diluting ownership may be undesirable for control reasons, and reacquiring shares may be impractical because there may be no sellers. Moreover, the 401(k) approach does not provide the Section 1042 "rollover" tax benefit that selling to an ESOP does in a C corporation, and the maximum amount that can be contributed is a function of how much employees put into savings. That will limit how much an employer can actually buy from a seller through a 401(k) plan to a fraction of what the ESOP can buy.

Despite these limitations, 401(k) plans are attractive as ownership vehicles where a company simply wants employees to become owners but has no need to buy out owners or use the borrowing features of an ESOP. A company can simply match employee deferrals with company stock or make a straight percentage of pay contribution to all employees eligible to be in the plan in the form of company stock.

The accounting treatment of 401(k) plans is straightforward; any corporate contributions are charged to earnings, while employee purchases of shares add to shareholder capital.

Designing an Equity Incentive Plan

Designing an individual equity plan requires a variety of issues to be considered. This section is not intended to provide specific guidelines on how to structure a plan but rather to raise the issues companies need to consider. In making these decisions, company leaders should consult with peers and advisors as well as evaluate available survey data on industry practices.

How Much to Share

The first decision is how much ownership to share. This issue will differ for closely held companies and public companies, so each kind of company is looked at separately.

Closely Held Companies

Except in an ESOP, where the goal is to sell stock to the plan, the most typical way a decision is made about how much ownership to share in a closely held company is for the current owner or owners to set aside an amount of stock that is within the maximum dilution level with which they are comfortable. This approach can create problems, however.

Typically, once this number is set, a large portion of those shares is either provided immediately to existing employees, or they are allocated to employees over a certain number of years. The problem with this strategy is that if the company grows faster than anticipated, there are no or relatively few shares left to give to new employees. That can be a severe problem in attracting and retaining good people. It can also create two classes of employees, some with large equity grants and some without them. Moreover, this model often does not create an explicit link between employee effort and the rewards of ownership.

A second approach focuses on what percentage of compensation it is necessary to provide in the form of equity in order to attract, retain, and motivate people. These decisions need to be based on a sense of what people can get elsewhere, as well as discussions with employees to get a sense of how much they expect.

Rather than thinking about "how much" in terms of a total percentage of company shares or total compensation, it might make sense to use a more dynamic model based on performance. In this approach, the issue for existing owners is not "what percentage of the company do we own," but "how much is what we own worth?" Owners in this model would rather own 10% of a $10 million company than 90% of a $1 million company. This notion can be made into an explicit plan by telling employees that if the company meets or exceeds certain targets, they will get a percentage of the incremental value created by that performance in the form of equity or something equivalent to equity, such as phantom stock. If the company exceeds its goals, then, by definition, sharing part of the surplus value leaves both the employees and the existing owners better off than they would have been. The targets can be anything—sales, profits, market penetration, or whatever else is critical to the company's future.

Closely held companies need to consider the possibility of making equity grants to so many employees that the grants create legal or regulatory problems. An S corporation, for instance, cannot have more than 100 shareholders, and option holders count as shareholders. If any corporation has more than 500 shareholders (an ESOP or 401(k) plan only counts as one, however), it becomes a de facto public company. Finally, equity plans may be subject to securities laws. This issue is described in more detail below in the section on securities law considerations.

Publicly Traded Companies

Publicly traded companies face many of the same design issues as their closely held counterparts and may want to use some of the same decision guidelines. Their principal constraint is investor concern about dilution. Dilution is usually measured by "overhang," the number of awards outstanding plus the number of shares available to be issued. This amount varies by company. In broad-based equity plans, we found that most companies fall in the 5% to 25% range, with very large public companies often in the lower end of the range and technology companies and younger companies in the higher end.

What Kind of Equity?

ESOPs are the vehicle of choice in closely held companies if an owner or owners want to use ownership sharing for business continuity. These plans also make sense in companies that have a strong commitment to sharing ownership broadly and find the ESOP rules acceptable given the tax benefits the plans provide. ESOPs do not work for companies that want to discriminate in terms of who gets awards or (in most cases) where the philosophy is that employees should have to buy stock to become owners. Section 401(k) plans make sense for companies that just want to share ownership broadly, are comfortable with the allocation rules, and, where employees are buying company stock, want to provide a tax-favored way to employees to invest. Generally, ESOPs and 401(k) plans are not means to provide incentives for individual behavior; instead, they are more targeted at providing incentives for employees as a group. ESPPs are a terrific benefit, but only a few companies will have active or substantial enough participation to make them a key element of their ownership cultures on their own. They are also less of an incentive plan than a way to reward employees.

Very small companies with no plans to be acquired or go public often want to use SARs or phantom plans because they are simple, do not require actual stock to be issued, and can be used to track equity changes in non-stock companies. They lack some of the connotation of ownership, however, and offer no favorable tax treatment. Stock options and restricted stock, by contrast, require that the company provide some form of liquidity for the shares, often through a public offering or sale, although companies can also simply arrange to repurchase the shares.

Restricted stock and restricted stock units deliver actual shares to employees, even if the stock price declines. There are pros and cons to this approach. On the one hand, employees do not end up with nothing just because share prices decline in the market generally. On the other hand, some have argued that restricted stock just provides "equity for breathing," and that it is thus less of an incentive than options or SARs. Restricted stock can cause more economic dilution than options or SARs (because options are only exercised if the price of the stock goes up), but it causes less dilution in terms of the number of shares outstanding. That is because the risk protection of restricted stock means that each share granted is worth more than each option or SAR. A ratio of one restricted stock share to three or four stock options is not uncommon, for instance.

Option plans can be just NSOs, just ISOs, or some of both. Most broad-based option plans provide NSOs for rank-and-file employees because few of these employees will be able or want to meet the buy-and-hold conditions of the ISO. Many of those who do want to hold onto the shares, moreover, will not get a large benefit from being able to pay capital gains taxes rather than ordinary income tax rates. Because the employees will not use the benefits of an ISO anyway, companies reason they might as well get the tax benefit of an NSO.

On the other hand, many plans aimed at highly paid employees are ISOs because these employees can greatly benefit from capital gains treatment, and they may demand such options to come to work for or stay with a company. All-ISO plans are also common in start-up companies where the company is not worried about tax deductions (because there are no profits) and thus is willing to give all employees the benefit of the doubt on the possibility of getting capital gains treatment on their options.

Who Is Eligible and Who Will Actually Get Equity?

In the past, the answer to the question of who is eligible was very simple for most companies: just the "key" people. In some ways, this is still how companies view equity; it is just that their definition of "key" has changed. For many companies, everyone is a key person. Many companies are pushing down more decision-making to all levels of the company, asking employees to make business decisions on a regular basis. Management at these companies reasons that if they want people to think and act like owners, they should make them owners. At the same time, for some companies in some labor markets, it is necessary to provide options at all levels just to attract and retain people.

For companies in these situations, the answer to "who's eligible?" is simple—everyone is. Other companies choose a more complex approach, however. There are several criteria that can be considered in making this decision. This discussion is only for plans other than ESOPs, 401(k)s, and ESPPs, where there are specific rules about eligibility. This discussion will only be about individual equity plans because, as explained above, these decisions are very constrained in ESOPs, 401(k)s, and ESPPs.

Tenure

At the simplest level, companies can require that people can get equity only after they have worked a minimum amount of time, often one year. This assures at least some commitment on the part of the employee to the company.

Full-Time/Part-Time

In the past, it was unusual to provide equity to part-time employees. Innovators like Starbucks, however, have provided options to everyone, arguing that many of their part-time people would (or if properly rewarded could) be long-term employees.

When Equity Will Be Granted

Equity can be granted either according to some kind of merit judgment or on the basis of a universal rule, such as allocating annually or on the date of hire, promotion, or the achievement of an individual, group, or corporate objective. These methods are not mutually exclusive; many companies use a combination of these techniques.

A typical merit-based plan would provide work unit managers (or a single manager in a smaller company) with a number of awards that can be granted to employees in the group based on a performance appraisal. An alternative to individual merit judgments is to provide that a pool of equity awards will be given to a work team on the achievement of their own goals. Many companies, of course, will simply name specific individuals, usually top managers, who will get equity, but the company will define how much they get based on some merit assessment.

At the other end of the spectrum is an automatic formula based on compensation, seniority, promotion, or some other work-related, measurable construct. This can be for one employee or every employee. For instance, a number of larger companies provide all employees meeting basic service requirements with 10% of pay every year in stock options. The argument behind these formulas is that compensation reflects management's judgment of an employee's contribution to the company, and equity is simply another form of compensation.

Providing awards on hiring, with additional grants on promotion or periodic refresher grants, is another common allocation rule. Linking additional grants to promotion gives employees an incentive to improve their skills and rewards those people the organization believes are making greater contributions. On the other hand, it can lose the attention of employees who may be very good performers but who are not in jobs that can easily lead to a promotion.

Refresher grants give employees additional awards when they exercise some of the options or other equity benefits they were previously granted. For instance, if an employee has 1,000 options and exercises 200, then the employee would be given new options on another 200 shares at exercise. The theory here is to maintain a constant level of equity interest in the company. Similarly, refresher awards might be granted when the company issues additional shares so that an employee maintains the same percentage of potential ownership as was held before the dilution (this feature would be more common for executive plans). While these automatic additional grants help to keep the employee's equity interest high, shareholders might object to the ongoing dilution.

How Often Should Awards Be Granted?

Equity inherently involves risk, but the design of plans can accentuate that risk. Companies that provide one-time grants or grants on the attainment of an event, such as hiring, promotion, or meeting some corporate target, place most or all of an employee's ownership interest in the company based on the price of stock at a single point in time.

This practice accelerates the risk of equity both for the employee and the company. With options and SARs particularly, equity granted at a high price may never be "in the money"; awards given at a low price may cost the company more than it ever intended when they are redeemed. Employees who happen to get their chunk of equity at a good time end up doing very well, while those who have gotten their grants when the price was not so favorable, don't do well at all. Creating an ownership culture of "we're all in this together" can be very difficult in these circumstances.

For many companies, the best way to deal with these potential problems is to provide grants in smaller amounts but more frequently. This works best for companies using equity as a compensation strategy. Start-ups whose stock value is close to zero anyway or who use large initial grants to attract people away from other opportunities may find this less appropriate. It also won't work for companies that want simply to make grants at the occasional discretion of the company, often on the attainment of some corporate milestone. These companies see equity more as a symbolic reward than as ongoing ownership strategy.

Smaller but more frequent grants are easiest to do in public companies where the share price is readily ascertainable and where share prices change continually. In a closely held company, there would be no point in granting equity more frequently than the stock is valued. Giving an employee a grant three times a year when the price per share is determined annually, for instance, would give the employee three sets of awards all at the same price.

The periodic allocation "dollar-cost averages" the awards, smoothing bumps in volatile markets. This approach also gives employees more of a long-term, ongoing stake in the company. With the vesting schedules attached to the repeated grants of awards, employees are provided an even longer-term interest in the company's performance. Finally, there will be fewer big winners and losers among employees with otherwise similar jobs.

Frequent grants are not all good news, of course. The more often awards are granted, the more complex their administration becomes. Even with the best software, there will be much more data entry, many more forms to file and disseminate, and many more errors that can be made.

When Will Employees Be Able to Use the Awards?

There are two principal issues in deciding when employees will be able to translate their equity into cash: vesting and exercise periods. Vesting generally provides that an employee accrues an increasing right to the awards granted based on the number of years worked. However, companies also sometimes use performance vesting, in which vesting is a function of company, group, or individual performance. As various targets are met, the equity awards becomes increasingly vested. The exercise period allows the employee to exercise or redeem an award for a defined number of years into the future once the award is vested.

The patterns on seniority-based vesting are fairly consistent across companies, with three to five-year graduated vesting the most common schedule. Sales or profit targets are the most common performance triggers. A more difficult decision is whether to provide for immediate vesting upon an event, such as going public or the sale of the company, even if the awards would not otherwise be vested. This clearly provides a good benefit for employees, but it may make it more difficult to sell a company or take one public, especially if buyers perceive that employees will now have fully vested options that, if they can also then be exercised, may be valuable enough so that some people will just walk away.

By far the most common exercise period for stock options is 10 years; there are no data on other plans. Some exercise periods are shorter, but they are rarely longer. There is nothing magical about 10 years for nonqualified options, but for incentive options, the exercise period cannot exceed 10 years. The more volatile a company's stock, the more important a longer exercise period is so that employees can weather the downturns. An alternative design used by a few companies allows employees to exercise their awards only when a defined event occurs, such as the achievement of a certain stock price or earnings goal. This accomplishes two things. First, it provides an incentive to meet the goal, and second, it reassures investors that dilution will only occur if the company meets certain targets. Once these targets are met, employees would normally be given a certain amount of time after the event to exercise the award, anywhere from a few months to several years. Alternatively, a company could provide that awards can only be exercised upon the occurrence of an event, such as a sale or going public.

In closely held companies, allowing exercise of an option or the right to sell shares only upon sale of the company or going public is a very common approach. If a company allows exercise and/or sale before then, employees end up owning stock and having a tax obligation. Unless the company can provide a market for the shares (an issue discussed below), this combination may not seem like much of a reward. Companies and employees have to weigh just how likely these events are to occur, however. Management is often excessively optimistic about how marketable their company is.

It is also important to consider, as with vesting, that if employees can exercise on sale or an IPO, buyers of the stock may not find the company so valuable. A minority of closely held companies are thus now restricting exercise to some time after a sale or an IPO (in a sale situation, this would require the acquiring company to provide options in the new employer).

Finally, the plan design should be specific in its compliance with applicable securities laws and stock exchange rules that can restrict certain employees from exercising equity awards or the sale of stock acquired from them by for a specified period after an IPO.

Providing a Market for the Shares

For publicly traded companies, providing a market for shares obtained through equity awards is not an issue, but for employees of closely held companies, it is one of the most important of all design issues. The majority of closely held companies solve the problem by limiting the exercise of equity awards to when the company is sold or goes public. This makes sense for companies who realistically see these alternatives as likely to happen in the foreseeable future. Some company leaders, however, assume that they can *only* provide for marketability upon these events because a closely held company, for one reason or another, cannot provide a market itself. There are, in fact, other alternatives. Moreover, some companies prefer to stay closely held. There are a variety of ways these companies can provide a market, including purchases by other employees (the company may act as a clearinghouse to let people know who is selling and who is buying), having the company buy back the shares, setting up an ESOP (which can buy the shares with pretax dollars through the ESOP trust) or, for companies willing to deal with the many securities law issues involved, setting up an internal stock market in which the company would act as a back-up buyer in a market it runs for employee buyers and sellers.

Premium Pricing and Other Performance Bells and Whistles

Some companies are now looking at adding more performance triggers to their individual equity plans. As mentioned, vesting can be performance-triggered, as can the actual grant of an award (or the size of that grant). In addition, companies can use premium-priced awards, such as issuing an option at a grant price 10% above the current market price. In the executive compensation field, there are entire books written about formulas to base equity awards on performance. Another idea growing in popularity is indexed awards, where the award either only vests or is granted if the company's stock outperforms its peers. The details of these approaches are beyond the scope of this chapter, however. Suffice it to say that a common problem is picking a performance measure (EBITDA, economic value added, stock price growth, etc.) that does not really capture either what the executive can actually make happen or what is best for the company overall, or both.

Securities Law Issues

If employees are given a right to purchase shares, the offer is subject to securities laws. ESOPs and 401(k) plans are not subject to most securities law requirements unless employees have a right to buy shares. The trust serves as the shareholder of record in these plans, and its ownership counts as one shareholder no matter how many people participate in the plan.

The two key elements of securities laws are registration and disclosure. Registration means the filing of documents with the state and/or federal securities agencies concerning the employer whose stock is being sold. There are registration procedures for small offerings of stock (under $1 million or $5 million, depending on the procedure) that can be done for relatively small legal fees (as little as $10,000 in some cases), but larger offerings require a lot of complex paperwork and fees often exceed $100,000. Registration requires the filing of audited financial statements and continuing reporting obligations to the federal Securities and Exchange Commission (SEC) and appropriate state agencies.

Disclosure refers to providing information to buyers about what they are getting, similar to, but frequently less detailed than, what would be in a prospectus. At times, there are specific state and federal rules about what needs to go in these documents, including objective discussions of risks, the financial condition of the firm, officers' and directors' salaries, and other information. In the absence of requirements for the registration of the securities, disclosure is intended to satisfy the anti-fraud requirements of federal and state laws.

Generally, offers to sell securities (stocks, bonds, etc.) require registration of those securities unless there is a specific exemption. In addition, corporations with 500 or more shareholders are considered public companies under federal law and must comply with the reporting requirements of the Exchange Act of 1934 even if they do not have to register under the Securities Act of 1933. For the purpose of counting shareholders, holders of unexercised options or restricted stock are included.

There are a number of exemptions from these rules. These are exemptions from registration; anytime stock is offered, it should include appropriate financial disclosure to satisfy anti-fraud rules.

The most important exemption is Rule 701. Under federal law, offers to a company's employees, directors, general partners, trustees, officers, or certain consultants (those providing services to a company similar to what an employer might hire someone to do, but not consultants who help raise capital) can be made under a written compensation agreement. If total sales during a 12-month period do not exceed the greater of $1 million, 15% of the issuer's total assets, or 15% of all the outstanding securities of that class, then the offerings are exempt from registration requirements. The offerings must be discrete (not included in any other offer) and are still subject to disclosure requirements. For total sales under $5 million during a 12-month period to the specified class of people above, companies must comply with anti-fraud disclosure rules; for sales over this amount, companies must disclose additional information, including risk factors, copies of the plans under which the offerings are made, and certain financial statements. These disclosures must be made to all shareholders.

For purposes of this rule, options are considered part of the aggregate sales price, with the option price defined as of the date of grant. In calculating outstanding securities for the 15% rule, all currently exercisable or convertible options, warrants, restricted stock, stock rights, and other securities are counted.

Other exemptions are available for sale to a limited number of accredited or sophisticated investors with appropriate information (these terms are legally defined and generally include officers, directors, and/or higher-income individuals); small offerings to 35 or fewer nonaccredited investors; offerings under $500,000; and offerings only to in-state residents if the offeror does 80% or more of its business and has 80% or more of its assets in-state.

These exemptions from registration are available under federal law. Some states track federal exemptions; some do not. Most states model their "blue sky laws" (the general name for state securities laws) on the Uniform Securities Act or the Revised Uniform Securities Act, which are partly based on federal law. Perhaps most importantly for offerings to employees, however, states that have a specific exemption parallel to the federal Rule 701 exemption (for offerings to employees) are the exception rather than the rule. State registration for such offerings may be needed, therefore, unless other exemptions are met.

Public companies cannot use Rule 701 for an exemption from securities law filings. Instead, most rely on Form S-8, a simplified registration form that can be used to comply with securities laws in conjunction with an offering of options. Public companies do not have to offer a formal prospectus to potential buyers, as closely held companies would. They are, however, required to provide information to employee stock purchasers about the company and its option plan. The S-8 form allows that to be done by reference to already available public documents.

Public companies must also make sure their plan design complies with trading restrictions that apply to corporate insiders. This requires the filing of various reports and the restriction of some trading activity, among other things. These issues are too technical for adequate discussion here. Public companies should consult with their legal counsel on these matters before designing a plan.

Chapter

5

Restricted Stock Plans

Restricted stock plans provide employees with shares of stock, contingent upon their continued employment with or service to the company or on the achievement of certain individual, group, or company performance targets. Employees may be required to purchase the stock or may receive it at no cost. This chapter discusses the characteristics, tax treatment, and accounting treatment applicable to these arrangements.

Characteristics of Restricted Stock Plans

A restricted stock arrangement provides the recipient with the right to acquire a specified number of shares of stock. The recipient may be required to pay for the stock or may receive it at no cost. If the stock must be purchased, the purchase price is typically the fair market value of the company's stock on the date of grant ("grant" here is used in its formal sense in a restricted stock plan and can refer to either the award of shares for no consideration or the award of the right to buy shares).

Privately held companies that offer restricted stock to their employees typically require the employees to pay full fair market value for the stock. While the company is private, the value of the stock is often relatively low, so that this price is not a significant obstacle to the employee's purchase, and requiring payment can alleviate administrative difficulties that might otherwise arise from the tax treatment of these arrangements. In addition, the employee's investment provides the company with additional cash that could be valuable to the operation of the company.

In a publicly held company, however, there is little incentive to employees to purchase restricted stock at full fair market value, since, presumably, they could buy the same stock on the open market at essentially the same price without regard to the restrictions. Because of this, publicly held companies that offer restricted stock to their employees typically offer it at no cost or at a discount from the current fair market value.

Unlike employee stock options, which might provide up to 10 years for employees to purchase stock, the recipient of restricted stock must make a decision with respect to acquiring the shares of stock within 10 to 30 days after the arrangement is granted. Where payment for the shares is required, generally the recipient may purchase the shares of stock with cash, a promissory note, or other consideration approved by the company.

Alternatively, the company may simply award restricted stock at no cost to employees. If the stock is awarded at no cost, it may be issued at grant subject to restrictions or may be awarded in the form of units that convert to shares of stock (usually on a one-for-one basis) upon distribution to the recipient.

In both publicly and privately held companies, the arrangement is granted subject to restrictions or risk of forfeiture. That is, the recipient's right to the shares of stock covered by the restricted stock arrangement (i.e., the "restricted shares") is contingent on continued service or contribution to the company for a specified period of time (the "vesting period"). Alternatively, the recipient's right to the restricted shares may be contingent upon the achievement of one or more specified performance goals.

If shares are issued at grant, the restricted shares are not transferable and are usually held by the company in an escrow or custodial arrangement during the vesting period. The recipient may have some of the rights of a shareholder with respect to the restricted shares during the vesting period, including the right to vote and to receive dividends. If the recipient fails to satisfy the vesting conditions (for example, by terminating employment before the completion of the vesting period or failing to achieve the performance targets), the company has the right to repurchase any unvested (unearned) restricted shares at a price equal to the shares' initial cost to the recipient. If, at the time of forfeiture, the shares are worth less than the recipient's initial investment, the repurchase price is typically the current fair market value of the stock. This repurchase right lapses cumulatively over the vesting period.

If the award is granted in the form of units, no shares are issued until the units are converted into stock (upon distribution to the recipient). The recipient does not have voting or dividend rights with respect to the underlying stock until this time (although some companies pay dividend equivalents on unvested units). If the recipient fails to satisfy the vesting requirements, the units are simply forfeited with no payment to the recipient.

Table 5-1 (see next page) compares the various forms of restricted stock.

The characteristics of restricted stock plans may be summarized as follows:

- Employees are generally required to accept awards or purchase shares (if payment is required), within 10 to 30 days of grant.

- If offered by a privately held company, the purchase price is usually at or near the fair market value of the company's stock on grant date. If offered by a publicly held company, the shares are usually awarded at no cost or at a discount.

- Shares or units are usually subject to vesting restrictions. If shares are issued at grant, they are usually held in escrow until vested.

- Upon termination of employment, unvested shares are forfeited or subject to repurchase at the employee's original cost.

- Both purchases and awards (of both stock and units) are generally subject to tax upon vesting, at which time the difference between the purchase price (if any) and the fair market value of the stock is treated as compensation income to the employee.

Table 5-1. Comparison of Various Forms of Restricted Stock

Restricted Stock Purchase	Restricted Stock Award	Restricted Stock Units
Price is typically equal to market value at grant.	Price is typically $0 or a nominal amount.	Price is typically $0 or a nominal amount.
Shares are issued at grant and held in escrow until vested.	Shares are issued at grant and held in escrow until vested.	Shares are not issued until distribution.
Underlying shares are considered issued and outstanding before vesting.	Underlying shares are considered issued and outstanding before vesting.	Underlying shares are not considered issued and outstanding until distribution.
Recipient has voting rights even before vesting.	Recipient has voting rights even before vesting.	Recipient does not have voting rights until distribution.
Recipient typically receives dividends on unvested shares.	Recipient typically receives dividends on unvested shares.	Recipient does not receive dividends on unvested units but may earn dividend equivalents.
Section 83(b) election can be filed at grant.	Section 83(b) election can be filed at grant.	Section 83(b) election is not applicable.
Taxation cannot be deferred beyond vesting.	Taxation cannot be deferred beyond vesting.	Taxation can be deferred beyond vesting if distribution of underlying shares is deferred (either mandatorily or through a valid deferral election).

- If shares are issued at grant, an election under Section 83(b) of the Internal Revenue Code (the "Code") can be filed at the time of purchase or award. If a Section 83(b) election is filed, the difference, if any, between the purchase price and the fair market value of the company's stock on the purchase or award date is compensation income to the employee. No taxable income is recognized on the vest date.

- If the award is made in the form of units, it may be possible to defer payment of income tax by deferring distribution of the underlying shares. The deferral and distribution is subject to Section 409A of the Code, and employment taxes (FICA and FUTA) will still be due upon vesting.

- Withholding tax obligations arise at the time compensation income is recognized.

- The company receives a tax deduction equal to the compensation income recognized by employees.

Advantages of Restricted Stock

From the company's perspective, restricted stock arrangements have many of the strengths of employee stock options. They enhance the company's ability to recruit and retain talented employees. They may be granted to specific individuals in different amounts and subject to different terms and conditions, enabling the company to tailor the arrangements to meet specific corporate objectives. If the arrangements require an immediate purchase of stock, they result in cash inflow to the company (assuming that the employees do not tender payment in the form of a promissory note or previously acquired shares of stock). The company may receive a corporate tax deduction (for compensation expense) when the restricted shares vest. And, as with other equity arrangements, restricted stock arrangements allow the company to align the interests of the employees with those of its shareholders.

For employees, restricted stock provides a relatively low-risk way to acquire and maintain an equity interest in the company. It may provide a strong motivational tool, as employees recognize that their individual performance can directly affect the company's prospects and, therefore, the value of the company's stock.

Advantages Distinct to Restricted Stock Issued at No Cost

Restricted stock that is awarded at no cost offers a distinct advantage over employee stock options and stock appreciation rights in that, regardless of fluctuations in the company's stock price, it always retains some value. Employee stock options and stock appreciation rights have little value (and do little to retain and motivate employees) when the current value of the company's stock is less than the option price. This disadvantage does not apply to restricted stock that is awarded at no cost; because employees have not paid for the stock, whether the company's stock price increases or decreases, the restricted stock always has value to them.

Some practitioners believe that restricted stock awarded at no cost provides a better incentive for long-term growth since these arrangements are not as leveraged as stock options (and therefore do not benefit as much from short-term spikes in stock value).

Finally, some practitioners believe that employees place a higher value on stock that they receive at no cost than they do stock options or stock appreciation rights, which inherently involve more risk. Where this is the case, restricted awards can be significantly smaller than stock options, reducing the company's overall expense for the plan (even though the per-share expense may be greater than for stock options) and plan dilution.

Disadvantages of Restricted Stock

There also can be drawbacks to using restricted stock arrangements as a compensation tool. The grant of restricted shares gives rise to a compensation expense if the purchase price is less than the fair market value of the company's stock on the date of purchase. If the shares are awarded at no cost, then the entire value of the grant is treated as a compensation expense. Moreover, if the recipient files a Section 83(b) election in connection with the purchase of the restricted shares at fair market value, the company may forego a compensation expense deduction for income tax purposes. And, as with any equity arrangement, the issuance of restricted stock will dilute the interests of the company's shareholders.

If employees are required to pay for the restricted stock, employees are making an immediate investment decision, and assuming the risk of a decline in the value of the stock before the stock is transferable. Employees may be unwilling to make this investment (especially when their ability to sell the stock is restricted subject to vesting requirements) and may incur substantial risk by doing so. Moreover, if the granting company is privately held, the restricted shares will be illiquid, further limiting the employee's ability to realize any appreciation in the value of the shares.

Unlike employee stock options, restricted stock arrangements offer employees little control over when the stock is subject to taxation. If a Section 83(b) election is not filed, each vesting date under the arrangement is a taxable event to the employee. Upon vesting, employees recognize compensation income equal to the difference, if any, between the purchase price of the restricted shares and the current fair market value of the company's stock, with a commensurate withholding tax obligation. Only with an award in the form of units is there any opportunity for the employee to defer taxation past vesting, and even there the deferral is severely limited by new Section 409A of the Code. The stock may vest at a time when the employee is already in a higher than normal tax bracket or when the employee does not have cash available to pay the withholding taxes. In some cases, employees may be forced to sell some of the restricted shares to satisfy this tax liability. When vesting occurs during blackout periods or other periods where employees are not able to sell the stock, satisfying the tax liability can be particularly problematic for employees. For companies that offer restricted stock at no cost, collecting the requisite tax withholding and assisting employees with their tax obligations is often one of the most significant administrative challenges that must be overcome; this is especially true when the plan is offered to a large group of employees.

Restricted Stock Plan Design

When a company decides to implement a restricted stock program, management usually instructs the human resources department and/or benefits personnel to design an appropriate plan. Typically, the plan's structure, as well as specific terms and conditions, are determined in consultation with the company's legal counsel, accountants, and outside compensation or benefits specialists. Factors taken into consideration in designing the plan include the cost to the company and proposed participants, the potential liquidity for participants, and the income tax and financial accounting consequences arising from the operation of the plan.

Some companies adopt a separate plan, under which only restricted stock can be offered; other companies adopt "omnibus" plans, under which a variety of equity vehicles, including restricted stock, can be offered. The omnibus plan clearly provides the company with maximum flexibility, allowing the company to determine what types of arrangements to actually offer to employees as the arrangements are granted. Unfortunately, shareholders are sometimes uncomfortable with this approach, and where shareholder approval is necessary or desired, the company may find it advisable to implement a separate plan for the restricted stock program.

In most cases, the company's legal counsel prepares the actual plan documents. Once management has approved the restricted stock plan, it is presented to the company's board of directors for consideration and adoption. Under the corporate laws of most states, the board has the authority for all issuances of the company's stock, so board approval is generally required before implementing a restricted stock plan.

Following adoption by the board of directors, the plan is usually submitted to the company's shareholders for approval. Shareholder approval may be a requirement under state corporate law or the company's charter documents. If the company is publicly traded, shareholder approval is almost always required by the exchange where the company's shares are listed. Even where shareholder approval is not required, there may be advantages to obtaining shareholder approval of the restricted stock plan for tax and/or securities law reasons.

Most restricted stock plans expressly provide that the board of directors can amend the plan from time to time, or even suspend or terminate the plan before the expiration of the plan term. Any such action is typically accomplished through a formal board resolution and results in an appropriate revision of the restricted stock plan document.

The restricted stock plan may expressly provide that certain types of plan amendments must be approved by the company's shareholders before becoming effective. These include amendments to increase the number of shares of stock authorized for issuance under the plan, to change or expand the categories of eligible participants in the plan, to extend the term of the plan, to reduce the purchase price at which shares of stock may be sold under the plan, or to increase the benefits available to participants in the plan. Even if not expressly required in the plan, it may be necessary to submit certain amendments for shareholder approval to ensure compliance with relevant laws or listing requirements.

Plan Participation/Eligibility

Restricted stock arrangements are not subject to statutory eligibility restrictions. Therefore, restricted stock can be offered to non-employees—such as outside directors, consultants, advisors, and other independent contractors—as well as to employees (both full-time and part-time), subject only to any eligibility restrictions contained in the restricted stock plan itself. Moreover, restricted stock can be offered pursuant to a restricted stock plan or as individual arrangements outside any formal plan.

Under a restricted stock plan, both the selection of recipients and the timing of grants are typically at the discretion of the board of directors. Companies use a wide variety of different approaches and/or policies for determining which employees should receive restricted stock. In some instances, only senior management is eligible to receive restricted stock. Other companies grant restricted stock to some or all managers. Still other companies grant restricted stock to all employees, regardless of job description.

Number of Shares Granted

Under a restricted stock plan, the number of shares of stock offered to each employee is typically determined by the board of directors. Companies use a wide variety of different approaches and/or policies to determine the size of a restricted stock arrangement. For example, the number of shares of stock may be determined on an employee-by-employee basis, by job classification or based on the company's overall performance over a specified period of time. The number of shares of stock may also be determined as a percentage of the employee's annual salary.

Purchase Price

Restricted stock can be offered at no cost or employees can be required to pay for the stock. If required to pay for the stock, the price can be the full fair market value of the stock or can be discounted. Typically, privately held companies offer restricted stock at a purchase price equal to the fair market value of the company's stock on the date of grant. Publicly held companies usually offer restricted stock at no cost or at a discounted price.

Expiration

If the stock must be paid for, employees typically have a limited period of time in which to complete the purchase. Typically, a decision to acquire the restricted shares must be made within 10 to 30 days after the restricted stock purchase arrangement is granted.

Although not legally required when the restricted stock is offered at no cost, for administrative purposes, the company may require employees to accept the offer of stock within 10 to 30 days after the offer is made. While the company could forego requiring acceptance from employees in this situation, it may be advisable to require employees to acknowledge the terms and conditions under which the stock is offered.

Vesting

The process of earning the restricted shares is commonly referred to as "vesting." Generally, a vesting schedule provides that, at the completion of designated intervals, or the satisfaction of established performance criteria, a pre-determined percentage or ratio of the restricted shares are earned and thereafter may be transferred by the employee. These interim dates are called "vesting dates." Vesting is typically measured from the date the restricted stock is granted, but it can be measured from any date the company deems appropriate (such as an employee's hire date).

Companies adopt a vesting schedule that best suits the incentive or other objectives of their restricted stock plan. Most restricted stock plans provide for annual vesting schedules; that is, the restricted shares vest in equal annual installments over a period of several years (typically, three, four, or five years). In some instances, monthly or quarterly vesting schedules are used, but because the administrative process of assessing and collecting the taxes that become due as the shares vest can be burdensome, companies may want to avoid vesting schedules where the shares vest in frequent intervals. Where restricted stock is offered at no cost to employees, frequent and/or short-term vesting is often viewed negatively from a corporate governance perspective. It is not uncommon for restricted stock issued at no cost to be subject to a three- to five-year vesting period, with no portion of the award vesting until the end of this period.

Restricted awards also can vest upon the achievement of specified company performance goals (such as earnings per share, revenue, or profitability targets) or based on work unit, individual, departmental, or divisional performance goals.

Termination of Employment

If an employee terminates employment before the restricted shares have vested, the unvested shares or units are typically forfeited or subject to repurchase by the company. Generally, the terms and conditions of forfeiture and the company's unvested share repurchase right are set forth in the restricted stock agreement. Where repurchase is necessary, the company usually must notify the employee in writing within a specified period of time (60 to 90 days following termination is common) of its decision to repurchase some or all of the unvested shares. To avoid a situation where the notice of repurchase is inadvertently overlooked, some plans provide that the company's repurchase option in automatically exercised unless the recipient is notified otherwise with a specified period (usually 60 to 90 days following termination).

If the employee originally paid for the stock, the company generally repurchases the stock at the lower of the employee's original cost or the current fair market value, since guaranteeing repurchase at the employee's original cost can negatively affect the accounting treatment of the plan (and, where the stock has declined substantially in value, could be a disincentive for continued employment). This payment is made in cash or by cancellation of any outstanding indebtedness of the employee to the company. Where the employee received the stock at no cost, any unvested shares are simply forfeited upon termination, with no payment from the company.

Additional Restrictions

Privately held companies occasionally impose restrictions on the ability of employees to transfer or dispose of vested restricted shares. These restrictions are intended to discourage employees from leaving the company, and to enable the company to maintain some control over the identities of its shareholders. Such restrictions may also enable the company to regulate and control the development of a trading market in its securities before its initial public offering.

One common type of transfer restriction is a "right of first refusal." A right of first refusal entitles a company to repurchase restricted shares of stock from the employee on the same terms offered, and at their current fair market value, if the employee proposes to sell or transfer the shares to a third party. Typically, the terms and conditions of a right of first refusal are set forth in the restricted stock agreement. A right of first refusal usually terminates when the company's securities become publicly held.

Another device used by privately held companies to restrict the transfer of shares of stock is a vested share repurchase right. As in the case of an unvested share repurchase right, this provision entitles the company to repurchase any vested shares of stock from an employee upon termination of employment. This allows the company to restrict share ownership to current employees and, provided the repurchased shares are returned to the plan, increases the number of shares the company has available to compensate current employees. On the other hand, employees may feel that once they have earned the stock, they should be entitled to keep it upon departure, and, particularly where the restricted stock serves as a substitute for other forms of compensation, may view this restriction unfavorably. If the company does choose to repurchase the vested shares, generally, the repurchase price is an amount equal to the fair market value of the company's stock on the date of termination of employment. Typically, the terms and conditions of a vested share repurchase right are set forth in the restricted stock agreement. A vested share repurchase right usually terminates when the company's securities become publicly held.

Other repurchase provisions may be triggered upon the death of the employee or in the event of a dissolution of marriage.

Tax Treatment

As is true of most arrangements that provide for the receipt of stock in connection with the performance of services, Section 83 of the Code governs the tax treatment of restricted stock arrangements. Because restricted stock is subject to Section 83 and because it is paid out immediately upon vesting, it generally is not treated as deferred compensation under Section 409A of the Code (enacted under the American Jobs Creation Act of 2004).

Note, however, that restricted stock units, which represent an unsecured promise to deliver stock at a future date, are treated as deferred compensation under Section 409A. Where the units are subject to distribution (and therefore, taxation) upon vesting, there should not be any adverse consequences under Section 409A. If the units are subject to deferred distribution, i.e., the units will be paid out some time after they have vested (either mandatorily or via a deferral election), it is critical for the arrangement to comply with the requirements in Section 409A governing both deferral elections and distributions. A full discussion of Section 409A is beyond the scope of this chapter, and much guidance is still anticipated regarding its application; therefore, companies that wish to offer restricted stock units, especially units subject to deferred distribution, are strongly encouraged to consult qualified tax advisors before proceeding.

Tax Treatment of Employee

Since the restricted shares are, by their terms, not transferable on the date of purchase or award and subject to a substantial risk of forfeiture (that is, the restricted shares are not vested), there is no taxable event at this time, and the compensatory element of the transaction remains open until the restricted shares vest. As the forfeiture restrictions lapse (that is, as the restricted shares vest), the difference—if any—between the purchase price and the fair market value on the date of vesting is compensation income to the employee. If the shares were awarded at no cost to the employee, this means that the full fair market value of the stock as it vests is compensation income to the employee. This compensation income is subject to taxation at ordinary income rates. As with other forms of compensation, such as salary and bonus, the employee must include the compensation income arising from the restricted stock in his or her ordinary income calculation for the year of vesting. The employee may elect to close the compensatory element of the transaction and accelerate the time at which compensation income is realized to the date of purchase or award by filing a Section 83(b) election with the IRS.

Where the restricted shares have been purchased at the full fair market value of the company's stock on the date of grant, generally the employee will make this election and recognize zero compensation income. If the restricted stock was awarded at no cost to the employee or purchased at a discount, filing a Section 83(b) election causes the employee to recognize compensation income equal to the full fair market value of the stock on the date of award or the amount of the purchase discount. This compensation income is subject to taxation at ordinary income tax rates and must be included in the employee's ordinary income calculation for the year. In the absence of an election, the compensatory element of the arrangement is not determined until the date of vesting, as described above. If a Section 83(b) election is filed and the employee subsequently leaves the company before the restricted shares have been fully earned, the employee is not entitled to a refund of the taxes paid at the time of award or purchase, nor is the employee entitled to take a loss deduction for the amount, if any, previously included in income. Likewise, if the stock declines in value after the award or purchase so that the fair market value of the stock upon vesting is less than the fair market value of the stock when the award or purchase occurred, the employee is not entitled to claim a loss deduction unless the shares are sold at the lower value. Thus, where the stock is purchased at a discount or awarded at no cost, filing a Section 83(b) election could cause employees to pay a higher amount of tax than if the election were not filed; few employees choose to file a Section 83(b) election in this situation. But where the employee is paying full fair market value to acquire the restricted stock, many employees do choose to file the Section 83(b) election, since, in this situation, it eliminates any compensation income associated with the arrangement.

The following examples may help clarify the tax treatment.

Example 1: Restricted Stock Purchased at Fair Market Value: An employee is offered the right to purchase 1,000 shares of restricted stock at a price of $10 per share, the fair market value on the date of grant. The stock vests in full one year after the date of grant, when the fair market value is $16 per share. In this example, if the employee does not file the Section 83(b) election, the employee recognizes compensation income of $6,000 in the year the stock vests. If the employee files the Section 83(b) election, the employee does not recognize any compensation income on the stock, since the purchase price is equal to the fair market value at the time the shares are purchased. In this example, the employee would most likely file the Section 83(b) election since it does not present any disadvantages to him or her.

Example 2: Restricted Stock Awarded at No Cost: An employee is awarded 1,000 shares of restricted stock at no cost when the fair market value of the stock is $10 per share. The stock vests in full one year after the date of grant, when the fair market value is $16 per share. If the employee does not file the Section 83(b) election, the employee recognizes compensation income of $16,000 in the year the award vests. If the employee files the Section 83(b) election, the employee recognizes $10,000 of compensation income in the year the stock is awarded, but does not recognize any additional income upon vest. Even in this example, it might be advantageous for the employee to file the Section 83(b) election, since doing so would reduce the amount of compensation income the employee would recognize for the award. But it is impossible for the employee to know that this is the case at the time the shares are awarded to him or her, which is when the Section 83(b) election must be filed. The employee could terminate employment before the vest date, forfeiting the shares, or the stock could subsequently decline in value. Thus, in this example, it is unlikely that the employee would file the Section 83(b) election.

Generally, restricted stock units are subject to the same tax treatment as restricted stock awarded at no cost, with a few important exceptions arising from the fact that stock is not issued at grant under a unit award. For an award to be subject to Section 83, a transfer of property must occur. Because there is no stock issued at grant under a unit arrangement, a transfer of property is not considered to have occurred at grant. Thus, unit awards are taxed under Sections 451 and 409A of the Code rather than Section 83. The first consequence of this treatment is that a Section 83(b) election is not available for unit awards. Some companies consider this to be an advantage, since, as discussed above, it is often inadvisable for employees to file a Section 83(b) election on restricted stock awarded at no cost, yet explaining the election can be cumbersome and confusing to employees.

The second consequence is that the recipient of a unit award does not recognize income until he or she has constructively received the compensation paid under it. If the unit is converted to stock and paid out at vesting, constructive receipt occurs at vesting, and the employee is taxed in exactly the same manner as if he or she had received restricted stock issued at grant that was not subject to a Section 83(b) election. If, however, the units are not converted to stock and paid out until some time after vesting, the employee is not subject to income tax until the actual distribution (note, however, that employment taxes, i.e., FICA and FUTA, are still due upon vesting), provided that the deferral and distribution comply with Section 409A.

The ability to defer distribution is also often perceived as an advantage of unit awards, and many companies offer employees the opportunity to elect a deferred distribution. Where this is offered, however, care should be taken to ensure that the deferral feature does not cause the plan to become subject to ERISA. This can particularly be a concern when distribution is deferred to the termination of employment, and it and may necessitate limiting the deferral feature to high-level employees. In addition, as previously mentioned, any deferral elections must now comply with Section 409A. Under the proposed regulations issued in September 2005, where restricted stock units do not vest for at least one year after grant, the initial deferral election can be made within 30 days of the grant date (provided that the election is made at least one year in advance of when the units are fully earned). Where restricted units vest in less than one year after grant, it may be necessary for the initial deferral election to be made before the end of the calendar year preceding the year in which the units are granted. Note, however, that as of the writing of this chapter, these regulations have not yet been finalized and are subject to change. In addition to regulating initial deferral elections, Section 409A also imposes limitations on when and how deferral elections can be changed and on re-deferrals. Finally, whether the deferred distribution is mandatory or elective, the distribution itself must comply with the requirements of Section 409A.

Employee Tax Withholding

If the recipient is an employee, any compensation income recognized in connection with a restricted stock purchase, award, or unit arrangement is subject to federal and state withholding obligations for income and employment tax purposes. Relevant withholding taxes include:

- Federal income tax
- Social Security
- Medicare
- State income tax (if applicable)
- State disability or unemployment (if applicable)
- Local taxes (if applicable)

For federal income tax purposes, any compensation income recognized for restricted stock is treated as a supplemental wage payment. This payment is eligible for withholding one of two ways. First, the compensation income may be aggregated with the employee's regular salary payment for the period, with withholding computed on the total amount. Alternatively, the compensation income is eligible for withholding at the flat rate for supplemental wage payments.

In addition, employment taxes under the Federal Insurance Contributions Act (FICA) and the Federal Unemployment Tax Act (FUTA) may be due. FICA is made up of two separate taxes: old age, survivor, and disability insurance (Social Security) and hospital insurance (Medicare). The Social Security component of FICA is collected up to an annual maximum. The Medicare component is collected against the employee's total earnings. The employer must match these taxes. The FICA rates and their applicable ceilings, if any, are subject to change annually. The company's payroll department should be contacted for notification as to when these rate changes occur.

Under Section 6672 of the Code, a 100% penalty may be imposed for failing to withhold and pay over taxes. There is no withholding required from a non-employee.

In the case of restricted stock purchases and awards, the withholding obligations arise at the time of vesting (or grant, if a Section 83(b) election is filed). Restricted stock units are subject to federal income tax withholding upon distribution (which may occur at vesting or later, if the unit arrangement is subject to either a mandatory or elective deferral) and are subject to FICA withholding (Medicare and Social Security) and FUTA at the time of vesting (regardless of whether distribution occurs at that time).

The withholding taxes collected by the company are only an estimate of the employee's ultimate tax liability. It may be necessary for the employee to make additional quarterly tax deposits depending upon his or her personal tax situation (or to remit additional amounts owed when tax returns are filed).

In addition to the company's withholding obligation, the company must furnish an employee (or former employee) receiving restricted stock with a Form W-2 for the year of vesting (or grant or distribution) reporting the compensation income recognized as "wages." If the recipient is a non-employee, the compensation income is not subject to withholding but must be reported on a Form 1099-MISC for the year of vesting (or grant or distribution).

Most states follow the federal treatment for income tax purposes and may require withholding of state disability or unemployment taxes. Generally, state taxes are determined on the basis of the employee's state of residence. The company may also be required to withhold certain local taxes in addition to federal and state taxes.

Tax Treatment of Employer Company

The company receives a corporate tax deduction (for compensation expense) under Code Section 162 equal to the amount included as compensation income in the gross income of the employee. The company generally is able to take the deduction in the taxable year that includes the close of the taxable year in which the employee recognizes income.

Under IRS regulations, an employer is allowed a deduction only for the amount of compensation "included" in the employee's gross income. This "included" amount is the amount reported by the employee on an original or amended tax return, or the amount included in the employee's gross income as the result of an IRS audit.

The regulations stipulate that timely compliance with the Form W-2 or Form 1099 filing requirements, reporting the amount includible in the employee's income, is deemed "inclusion" of the amount in gross income. The employer company is not required to establish that the employee actually included the reported amounts in his or her income tax return. Where the amount of compensation income recognized meets the requirements for exemption from reporting for payments aggregating less than $600 in any taxable year, or is eligible for any other reporting exemption, no reporting is required in order for the employer company to claim the deduction.

In the case of restricted stock offered to the chief executive officer or one of the four most highly compensated executive officers of a publicly held corporation, the compensation income recognized by the employee is subject to the deduction limit of Section 162(m) of the Code. This limit is not applicable, however, if the restricted stock arrangement qualifies for the exception for "performance-based" compensation.

Disposition of Stock

Upon a sale or other disposition of the restricted shares, the employee generally recognizes a capital gain or loss equal to the difference between the employee's adjusted tax basis in the restricted shares and the sale price. An employee's tax basis in the restricted shares is equal to the total purchase price paid (if any) for the shares plus the amount of compensation income recognized by the employee. Generally, this means that the restricted shares have a tax basis equal to the fair market value of the company's stock on the date of vesting/distribution (or the date of grant, if a Section 83(b) election is filed).

For purposes of computing the holding period for long-term capital gains treatment, the holding period generally commences on the date of vesting. Where a Section 83(b) election is filed, however, the holding period commences on the date of grant or purchase, and where a unit award is subject to deferred distribution, the holding period commences on the date of distribution.

International Tax Considerations

Outside of the U.S., the tax treatment of restricted stock can vary greatly from country to country. Some countries assess income based on any value at the time of grant or purchase (regardless of vesting), but other countries may defer taxation until the arrangement vests or until the underlying shares are sold. In countries where restricted stock awards are taxed at grant (which is generally undesirable), this outcome may sometimes be avoided by granting restricted stock units instead. In some countries, it may be necessary for participants to complete filings with the local tax authorities to defer or accelerate the time at which the stock is taxed. The tax rates applicable to restricted stock may be substantially higher than the tax rates that apply in the U.S.

There may also be significant obligations imposed on the company for the restricted stock. The company may be required to fulfill reporting obligations for the income recognized by participants and may also be required to withhold taxes on this income. Where withholding is required, there may not be a flat withholding rate applicable to stock compensation (as exists in the U.S.), in which case companies will need to work closely with local payroll offices (or apply to the local tax authorities for a flat rate) to determine the appropriate tax withholding rates. Many countries also have substantial social insurance taxes that can apply to stock compensation, often with matching payments required from the company. In some cases, the company's matching payments may not be subject to any maximum and could ultimately become a significant burden for the company.

Many countries provide some form of qualified stock option that is subject to lower tax rates, yet only a few countries provide the same benefit to restricted stock arrangements. Thus, offering restricted stock could be significantly more costly to both participants and the granting corporation (which may have to make matching social insurance contributions that would not apply under a qualified option plan).

The company should review the tax treatment applicable to the plan in each country where it will be offered carefully with its legal advisors before offering restricted stock to any employees outside the U.S. Failure to comply with local laws could ultimately be very costly to the company; it can be difficult to correct errors or minimize the cost to the company after the stock has been granted.

Financial Statement Impact

The accounting treatment of restricted stock plans may have a direct effect on the company's financial results. Until now, companies have had two alternatives to account for stock compensation arrangements: APB Opinion No. 25 or FAS No. 123. In the near future, however, all companies will be required to adopt FAS No. 123 (and, in fact, many companies have already been required to adopt it).

Where service-based restricted stock is concerned, it makes little difference which standard a company relies on, as the expense associated with service-based restricted stock is generally the same under both standards. For restricted awards that vest subject to performance goals, FAS No. 123 might be the preferable standard.

For the short time remaining, if any, that companies can continue to rely on APB Opinion No. 25, however, the company must use the same standard to account for all of its stock plans; it cannot choose to selectively apply FAS No. 123 to its performance-based restricted award plan.

Accounting Principles Board Opinion No. 25

Under Accounting Principles Board Opinion No. 25 (APB Opinion No. 25), any employee stock plan considered "compensatory" in nature may give rise to a compensation expense that must be reflected in a company's financial statements. An employee stock plan is considered a compensatory plan unless the plan is (1) "nondiscriminatory," (2) requires that all participants receive equal treatment, (3) has an exercise period of "reasonable" length, and (4) offers purchase discounts which are not greater than would be reasonable to offer to stockholders and others. Since a restricted stock plan does not satisfy all of these criteria, it is considered to be a compensatory plan, requiring the recognition of compensation expense.

A compensatory restricted stock plan requires that the granting company record an income statement expense equal to the difference, if any, between the purchase price of the restricted shares and the fair market value of the company's stock on the "measurement date" (usually the date of grant).

The measurement date is considered to be the first date on which both the number of shares that the employee may purchase and the purchase price are known. For restricted stock arrangements where vesting is contingent only on continued service, the measurement date is the date that the arrangement is granted. If the restricted stock is subject to forfeiture based on the completion of performance targets, the measurement date is the date the performance targets are achieved.

Awarding restricted stock at no cost to employees or offering it at a purchase price less than the fair market value of the company's stock on the date of grant results in a compensation expense. This expense must be amortized, or "accrued," over the service period for the arrangement—generally, the vesting period (that is, the period over which the company receives the benefit of the employee's services). If the measurement date occurs after the grant date (as can be the case if vesting is contingent on performance criteria), the arrangement is subject to "variable-plan" accounting. Under variable-plan accounting, the amount of compensation expense that must be recorded is based on the fair market value of the company's stock at the end of each accrual period until the measurement date is reached.

Statement of Financial Accounting Standards No. 123

Effective for fiscal years beginning after December 15, 1995, Statement of Financial Accounting Standards No. 123, *Accounting for Stock-Based Compensation* ("FAS No. 123"), governs the financial statement impact of restricted stock plans. Restricted stock plans generally are accounted for under FAS No. 123 in the same manner that they are accounted for under APB Opinion No. 25 (i.e., the difference, if any, between the purchase price of the restricted shares and the fair market value of the company's stock on the "measurement date" is an expense to the company).

Under FAS No. 123, the measurement date is the date the terms of the arrangement are mutually understood by both the company and the employee. For restricted stock granted to employees of the company, this almost certainly is the date of grant. Even if the restricted stock is subject to forfeiture based on the completion of performance targets, the measurement date is generally still considered to be the date of grant. Because of this, if a company offers restricted stock that vests contingent upon performance, the company may find FAS No. 123 preferable to APB Opinion No. 25.

For restricted stock or units where vesting is contingent on continued service or performance goals that are not related to the company's stock price (such as earnings or revenue targets), the fair value of the arrangement is generally equal to its intrinsic value. Where dividends are paid on the underlying stock but will not be paid on the unvested restricted stock or units, the fair value can be reduced by the present value of the dividend stream that is expected to be paid to shareholders over the vesting period of the arrangement. For restricted stock where vesting is contingent on market conditions (e.g., stock price targets or shareholder return), the fair value is adjusted based on the probability that the targets will be met. This adjustment must be computed with an option pricing model.

For restricted arrangements granted to non-employees, with the exception of outside directors (who are treated as employees for accounting purposes), under EITF 00-19, the measurement date is typically the date the arrangement vests. Moreover, the company cannot rely on APB Opinion No. 25 for arrangements granted to non-employees (not even for the short time remaining before required adoption of FAS No. 123).

If the restricted stock is offered to employees at a price equal to the fair market value on the date of grant, the company does not recognize any expense for the arrangement. Where a company grants restricted stock purchase arrangements to employees with a purchase price less than the fair market value of the company's stock on the date of grant, or awards the stock at no cost to employees, compensation expense results under FAS No. 123. This expense must be amortized, or "accrued," over the service period for the arrangement. As under APB Opinion No. 25, the service period is generally the vesting period for the arrangement, but other factors, such as automatic acceleration of vesting upon retirement, may have an impact on the determination of the service period. Where the arrangement is subject to vesting contingent on performance goals or price targets, the service period is derived based on the time period in which the goals or targets are expected to be achieved.

Where restricted stock is subject to vesting that is contingent on service or non-market performance conditions, expense is accrued only for the portion of the arrangements that are expected to vest. If the expected or actual vesting outcome varies, the expense accrual is adjusted to reflect the new expected or actual outcome so that expense is recorded only for those awards that actually vest. Where restricted stock is subject to vesting that is contingent on market conditions, the expense is not adjusted for expected or actual forfeitures. Because the initial fair value of the arrangement is reduced to reflect the market conditions, expense is recorded for the arrangement regardless of whether those conditions are met.

Statement of Financial Accounting Standards No. 123(R)

As originally issued, FAS No. 123 permitted companies to continue to rely on APB Opinion No. 25 rather than adopting the expense recognition provisions included in FAS No. 123. Although there is little difference between APB Opinion No. 25 and FAS No. 123 with respect to service-based restricted stock (and FAS No. 123 might be considered the more favorable standard with respect to performance-based awards), many companies that offer restricted stock also offer stock options and, therefore, chose to continue to rely on APB Opinion No. 25 for as long as possible. These companies are required to disclose on a pro forma basis the impact FAS No. 123 would have had on income if they had adopted it.

In December 2004, the FASB issued FAS No. 123 (Revised) ("FAS 123(R)"). This revision of FAS No. 123 prohibits continued reliance on APB Opinion No. 25. Public companies must adopt FAS No. 123(R) in their first fiscal year beginning after June 15, 2005 (December 15, 2005, for small business issuers). Private companies that currently use the minimum value approach under FAS No. 123 must adopt FAS No. 123(R) by their first fiscal year beginning after December 15, 2005. Generally the accounting treatment applicable to restricted stock under FAS No. 123(R) is the same as under original FAS No. 123.

Disclosure

To accurately represent a company's financial condition and capital structure in its financial statements, certain disclosures are required under generally accepted accounting principles and the rules of the Securities and Exchange Commission. FAS 123(R) sets forth the specific financial statement disclosures that are required with respect to a company's employee stock option plan.

Under FAS 123(R), the following information must be disclosed about a company's restricted stock plans:

- A description of the restricted stock arrangements, including vesting conditions, price, and the number of shares authorized for issuance under the plan.

- The weighted average grant date fair value of arrangements granted under the plan.

- A description of the method used to calculate the fair value. Where restricted stock vests based on market conditions, this also should include a discussion of how the effect of these conditions on fair value was determined.

- The total compensation cost recognized for the company's equity compensation plans, including restricted stock.

- The remaining unrecognized compensation cost for the company's equity compensation plans, including restricted stock, and the period of time over which it is expected to be recognized.

- A description of any modifications to previously granted restricted stock arrangements, including the terms of the modifications, number of employees affected, and additional incremental cost resulting from the modification.

- The amount of cash received from payments for restricted stock and/or tax benefits realized by the company.

- The company's policy for issuing restricted stock, including the source of shares (i.e., authorized but unissued shares or treasury shares) and the number of shares the company expects to repurchase in the following annual period.

The company should provide the following additional information for restricted stock purchase and award plans:

- The number and weighted average grant date fair value of shares unvested at the beginning of the period.

- The number and weighted average grant date fair value of shares hares unvested at the end of the period.
- The number and weighted average grant date fair value of shares granted, vested, and forfeited during the period.

The company should provide the following additional disclosures for restricted stock units:

- The number and weighted average conversion ratio of units outstanding at the beginning of the period.
- The number and weighted average conversion ratio of units outstanding at the end of the period.
- The number and weighted average conversion ratio of units convertible at the end of the period.
- The number and weighted average conversion ratio of units granted, forfeited, or converted during the period.
- The number, weighted average conversion ratio, aggregate intrinsic value, and weighted average remaining term of units outstanding (for fully vested units and those expected to vest during the current period).
- The number, weighted average conversion ratio, aggregate intrinsic value, and weighted average remaining term of units currently convertible (for fully vested units and those expected to vest during the current period).
- The total intrinsic value of units converted during the period.

Accounting for Tax Effects

The expense that companies recognize for restricted stock differs from the tax deduction they are entitled to for the arrangements both in terms of timing and the amount of the tax deduction. The expense recognized for the arrangement is equal to the fair value of the arrangement (typically the intrinsic value of the underlying stock) at grant and is recorded over the arrangement's service period, typically the vesting schedule. The company's tax deduction, however is generally realized only once the arrangement vests (and, in the case of restricted stock units subject to deferral, not until the shares are released) and is equal to the intrinsic value of the stock at this time. These differences must be accounted for in the company's financial statements.

Assuming that a Section 83(b) election has not been filed for the award, the company records an estimated tax benefit (sometimes referred to as a deferred tax asset) as it recognizes expense for the award. This estimated benefit is always equal to the amount of expense recognized multiplied by the company's statutory tax rate (regardless of the current intrinsic value of the stock), and it reduces the company's reported tax expense. Upon realization of a tax deduction (at either vest or release of the shares), the actual tax savings resulting from the deduction is compared to the estimated benefit recorded earlier. Where the tax savings exceeds this benefit, the excess is recorded to additional paid-in capital. Where the tax savings is less than the previously estimated benefit, the shortfall is deducted from paid-in capital, provided that enough paid-in capital is available from the excess tax benefits recorded for prior stock plan transactions. Where insufficient paid-in capital is available from prior stock plan transactions, the shortfall is treated as additional tax expense.

For example, assume a company grants a restricted stock award for 10,000 shares when the market value of the underlying stock is $10 per share. The award vests in full two years after the date of grant, and the employee does not file a Section 83(b) election. The total expense for the award is $100,000 (10,000 shares multiplied by $10 per share). This expense is recorded over the two years that the award is vesting. During this same period, the company records an estimated tax benefit of $40,000 (assuming a combined statutory tax rate of 40%) and reduces its reported tax expense by this amount as well.

Now assume that the market value is $17 per share when the award vests. At this market value, the company recognizes a tax deduction of $170,000, which, at the same 40% tax rate, produces an actual tax savings of $68,000. This tax savings exceeds the previously estimated tax benefit by $18,000, which is treated as additional paid in capital (it does not further reduce the company's tax expense.

On the other hand, if the market value when the award vests is only $8 per share, the company's tax deduction will be only $80,000, and the resultant tax savings is only $32,000. This is $8,000 less than estimate benefit recorded for the award. In other words, the company reduced its reported tax expense by $40,000 for the award but only realized an actual tax savings of $32,000; thus, the tax reflected in its financial statements is less than the amount of tax actually paid. This $8,000 shortfall is merely deducted from paid-in capital, assuming enough exists from prior stock plan transactions. The amount of the shortfall that exceeds the paid-in capital that is available from prior stock plan transactions is treated as additional tax expense.

Where a Section 83(b) election is filed for a restricted stock purchase or award, there will generally be no difference between the expense recognized for the arrangement and the tax deduction realized for it. In addition, the company's actual tax savings will be known at grant; thus, there is no need to reduce tax expense based on an estimated amount. As expense is recorded for the arrangement, the company will simply reduce tax expense based on the amount of actual tax savings realized at grant. Assuming the company's tax deduction equals the expense recognized for the award, no adjustments to paid-in capital will be necessary.

Other Considerations

In addition to the issues raised above, companies must also pay close attention to securities laws, administrative issues, and, when plans are extended outside the U.S., international considerations such as labor laws and data privacy laws, all of which are beyond the scope of this chapter. These and other issues are explored in depth in the author's chapter on this subject in the book *Beyond Stock Options*, also published by the NCEO (the book also includes model plan documents).

Simulating Employee Ownership with a Rolling Bonus Program

Corey Rosen

For many very small businesses and for some larger ones, it is impractical or undesirable to set up a plan that actually shares stock with employees. There are a number of possible reasons for this. The company may be a partnership, sole proprietorship, or limited liability company (a kind of hybrid partnership/S corporation) and thus not have any stock to share. For S or C corporations, sharing stock is a possibility, but not necessarily a desirable one. The legal costs of setting up an ESOP (employee stock ownership plan) will almost always be prohibitive ($30,000 or more in most cases). A 401(k) plan in which the company contributes shares to employee accounts is unappealing in an S corporation because the plan would have to pay "unrelated business income tax" on its attributed share of corporate earnings. That tax could often be at the highest personal tax rate. Presumably, the company would have to make additional contributions to the plan to pay the tax (otherwise, the plan trustee would be imprudent to accept company stock as a contribution). A 401(k) plan with employer stock as a matching contribution from the company may make sense for a C corporation, although it would be necessary to have the shares valued each year to protect against potential employee lawsuits and IRS claims for improper deductions.

Some companies will consider selling stock to employees, but this requires them to purchase shares with after-tax dollars and may require financial disclosure statements, something many business owners find either too costly or too much an invasion of their financial privacy. Giving stock to employees can avoid these securities issues, but the gift would be taxable to the employee at the time of receipt, even though the employee may not be able to sell the shares for some time into the future.

Stock options or restricted stock may make sense for S or C corporations, but they raise potentially difficult issues. First, the company must provide a way employees can turn the shares they buy with their options into actual cash. Most companies offering options broadly envision being sold or going public to make this possible. Otherwise, companies must buy the shares back themselves or arrange a market among employees. This may be difficult to do in smaller companies. Salaries are typically lower, and employees may not, as a result, have as much discretionary income to buy out another owner with after-tax savings as would be the case with executives of larger organizations. Small companies are also less likely to have either the cash flow or access to credit that larger companies have to make a redemption possible. Second, when employees start exercising their options or restricted stock, companies must comply with at least the anti-fraud disclosure requirements of state and federal securities laws. The required statements to employees usually cost $15,000 or more to prepare and require detailed financial information to be shared. Finally, in some companies, explaining the complexities and uncertainties of stock options (how they work, how a price for options is determined, how they are treated from a tax standpoint, and so on) can be daunting.

Aside from all these practical considerations, some business owners are simply not comfortable with the idea of sharing actual ownership, usually because they fear a loss of control or potential future litigation from unhappy shareholders. Nonetheless, they want to provide an incentive for employees that is linked not to short-term profits or some limited measure of performance, such as sales increases or quality control, but instead to the growth of the company over an extended period of time. This article describes an approach that can accomplish this objective in a way that imposes the least risk and entails the lowest costs for both the employer and the employee.

Phantom Stock: Not Always as Good as It Seems

For many small company owners, phantom stock and its cousin, stock appreciation rights (SARs) often seem like the perfect solution to the equity sharing puzzle. In practice, however, phantom stock and SAR plans can also raise problems when used as a means of providing equity to most or all of a company's employees. In a phantom stock or SAR plan, employees would be given a payment in cash at the end of a designated period of time equal to what would be the value of a designated number of shares or, with SARs, the increase in that value.

For instance, an employee might be given 100 shares of phantom stock in Quantum Mechanics, a small automobile diagnostic shop. At the time of the gift, Quantum had 1,000 total shares outstanding. These shares would be assigned a value at the time of the award, usually by the board of directors. The value would commonly be based on book value or some formula related to earnings or cash flow (these formulas usually produce a value that is considerably different from what a more thorough and professional appraisal would produce). No actual shares would be transferred. At some point in the future, usually when the employee leaves, he or she would receive the current value of those 100 shares. In an SAR plan, the employee would receive just the increase in the value of the 100 shares. That value would be affected by the growth of the company and by how many additional shares the company has issued over the ensuing years.

Each time new shares are issued, the ownership interests of other owners are diluted, unless the value of the phantom shares or SARs is recalibrated. Properly structured, the employee should not have to pay tax at the time the phantom shares or SARs are awarded. When the cash payment is made later, it will be taxed as ordinary compensation and will be tax-deductible to the company.

If the company has no shares, employees can instead be given a phantom percentage of the total company equity.

This sounds like the perfect solution, but it raises potential difficulties. First, if the company actually puts money aside to pay for the phantom stock or SARs, it cannot take a tax deduction for these funds. Moreover, if the funds accumulate to a large enough amount, the company could be subject to an excess retained earnings tax. If the company does not set aside the money, employees may, with reason, not have much faith that they will ever actually get anything from this plan. Second, if the plan provides for phantom shares for most employees, the U.S. Department of Labor may claim that it is actually a retirement plan in disguise and must be subjected to the expensive regulations of retirement plans—but without any of the accompanying tax benefits. This has been a gray area of the law. It seems clear that a phantom plan or an SAR plan can be provided with few, if any, limitations for executives and key management of a company, as well as to selected employees. Some advisors argue that if the plan is structured so that it does not provide payouts at retirement or termination of employment, that suffices to be excluded from retirement plan rules. Other advisors are more cautious, however, saying that if the plan provides payouts well into the future, even for people still employed, it might be considered a retirement plan.

Phantom stock and SARs are also not appealing from an accounting standpoint; the company must accrue a charge against earnings for the accrued liability, adjusting the liability each year as stock value and the vesting of awards changes. Finally, the very name "phantom" can make getting employees enthused a difficult task. SARs may present less of a problem on this front, ironically, even though their benefit is less assured. The result of these considerations is that truly broad-based phantom stock or SAR plans are extremely rare.

The Rolling Equity Bonus:
A Simple Ownership Equivalent

By varying the phantom stock or SAR idea somewhat, we can create a system that should function smoothly. It would work much like an SAR except that, unlike most SARs, it is specifically designed to make an annual payout, and it is based on equity performance over a short period of time. The idea is to mimic what would happen if employees were given stock options. With a stock option, an employee has the right to buy a certain number of shares at a price fixed today for some number of years into the future. When the option is exercised and the shares are sold, the employee ends up with the spread between the grant price and exercise price. If the option were granted at $10 in 1998 and exercised and sold at $18 in 2004, the employee would get $8 net for each share. In the best-designed option plans, employees get new options each year, thus giving them an ongoing interest in the company. While some old options will be exercised at various times, employees will always have new ones to give them an interest in the company's future.

With the rolling equity plan, an employee instead gets a bonus to be paid at some future point based on the increase in the company's equity value. Each year, employees are given a promise for an additional bonus at a point further into the future. Because employees are not given an irrevocable right to a future benefit (their right to get paid in the future is subject the "significant risk of forfeiture" that they may not still be employed when the bonus is paid), the payout should be taxed as a compensation cost only when it is paid out. At that point, it would be treated like any other wages or bonuses.

The accounting treatment, however, is less clear. New accounting rules effective in 2005 will require companies to show a charge to earnings for all equity plans based on an estimation of their value at the time the award is granted, not when they are paid out. Awards settled in cash, rather than shares, would be accounted for by making an initial estimate of value, then adjusting it annually to reflect changes in the price of the shares and the vesting of the awards. The concept proposed here is tied to equity performance, but it is not yet clear whether the new rules will apply to cash bonuses that are paid out based on equity performance over short periods of time. Companies clearly could take the more conservative approach and account for the awards at grant, then make adjustments, however, even if they are not required to do so. For most closely held companies, these accounting considerations will not play a significant role in their decision.

An illustration makes the concept of the rolling equity clearer. Instead of issuing stock, in 1998, Quantum Mechanics tells employees they will get a bonus in 2001 based on a percentage of the increase in the equity value of the company over the trailing three years. This can be based on a book measure or a formula, such as one based on a price-to-earnings ratio. In 1999, Quantum would announce that in 2002, there will be another bonus if the equity value in 2002 exceeds the equity value in 1999 by a defined amount. This approach can continue in three-year increments every year. The bonus would be treated as compensation to employees in the year paid and would be deductible to the company at that time.

There are a number of variations on this theme, of course. For instance, a company could apply a vesting concept so that employees would only get the bonus in any year if they had been working for the company for the three prior years. The number of years being measured could be varied, and the bonus need not be given annually. There could be a trigger for the bonus, such as reaching a stated profit, sales, or retained earnings target. Obviously, the percentage of the growth in equity that is distributed can be whatever the company chooses and can change from year to year. The way the bonus is allocated is also optional; it might be based on relative pay, for instance, or some merit judgment.

If the company is sold, employees can get a share of the sale proceeds, provided the plan is designed appropriately. To do this, the plan should state that should the company be sold, employees will get the same share of the increase in equity value that results from the sale as they would have earned if a three-year period had elapsed.

This system has a number of advantages. Unlike other ownership plans, it does not require employees to wait until they leave the company or some other far off event to get a reward. In large, well-established companies, this is less of an issue because people can see a long-term career path, know the company has a track record, and are more easily convinced that a promised benefit will be paid. In newer and smaller companies, employees may not identify with the company's long term goals and may be more skeptical of the value of owning shares in the company. In the rolling equity plan, employees can be given a realistic time horizon to be paid, but still have a clear interest in helping the company grow long term.

A second advantage is that it gives the company a context in which to explain to employees what the numbers for the business mean and what they can do to reach them. That, after all, is the point: getting employees to understand how to think and act like business people.

Finally, the system is infinitely flexible and legally simple. It is nothing more than a bonus program that has somewhat different parameters than the usual annual Christmas bonus. It can be designed and implemented with relatively simple special legal advice. It would be desirable, however, to have a financial advisor help think through how an equity measure can be built and how much of the increment employees should get.

As a company grows or, if not an S or C corporation, becomes one, it may reach a point where the advantages of a formal employee ownership plan become more important. Employees will already understand the basic concepts of equity sharing, so the transition to actual stock, along with the usually considerable tax advantages a formal plan brings to them, should make this transition a smooth one.

Replacing Stock Options with Performance Shares

Matt Ward

There has been much discussion of how mandatory expensing under the new equity accounting standard, FAS 123(R), will affect companies that use stock options as equity incentives. However, requiring an earnings charge for stock options will not mean the end of the world. Companies have two courses of action to take in response that can maintain and perhaps even improve their motivational stock-based long-term incentive programs. One is simply to improve investor relations while maintaining existing equity compensation approaches. The second is to reopen the stock compensation toolbox to figure out a more economically effective strategy.

The Enhanced IR Approach

At one end of the spectrum of choices, companies can simply maintain the status quo and continue their current programs despite the accounting charge. While not required, it would behoove these firms to beef up their investor relations (IR) activities as they relate to communicating the true metrics of value creation for their businesses. Earnings charges for stock options are non-cash charges to earnings that have no impact on the true value-creating cash flows of a business enterprise. IR can begin to present comparative performance results, supported by supplemental SEC disclosures. These may indicate that the company's true performance on key value-based metrics is the same or better than peer companies and other investments competing for shareholder dollars, despite the poor performance that would be indicated by traditional earnings and EPS numbers due to an earnings charge for stock options granted in meaningful amounts to broad-based groups of employees.

Reopening the Stock Compensation Toolbox

Stock Options May Not Be the Best Incentive

At the other end of the spectrum, companies may want to take a step back and reevaluate their choices when it comes to stock-based long-term incentives in an era where stock options have a charge to earnings. Stock options are the most prevalent stock-based long-term incentive. They are not the best incentive. Options can have value when individual or company performance is poor, and they can be worthless when individual or company performance is excellent. Their prevalence is due to favorable financial characteristics that existed under the old accounting rules and to the major cash inflows they created. Those accounting rules, by the way, were sound and based on long experience of a positive nature. Politics and misdirected outrage toward criminal executive behavior have made stock option accounting the unfortunate whipping boy of corporate governance reforms. The old accounting rules reflected the cost of options through the denominator of the EPS equation and through built-in controls like preapproval of maximum potential dilution amounts by the shareholders, the board of directors, or both. Nonetheless, the accounting rules have changed, and the financial advantages of options are now outweighed by their disadvantages and poor incentive characteristics.

Performance Shares Emerge as the Most Prevalent and Best Incentive

In an options expensing world, performance shares emerge as the best alternative for stock-based long-term incentives and will in all likelihood replace options as the most prevalent incentive. Why is that? The ultimate value of performance shares is tied to both the external stock price (thus aligned with shareholders' objectives) *and* internal or externally based measures of performance (thus aligned with management objectives). More importantly, performance shares have value from the date of grant and thus are unlikely to go underwater. As a result, it takes fewer shares to deliver competitive long-term incentive values. Under most assumptions, the value of grants under a performance share program can replace an existing option program and use 25% to 50% of the shares needed for options. Obviously, this would result in a dramatic reduction of overhang and net run rates for long-term incentives, which would make shareholders very happy. For example, assume the facts in table 7-1.

Table 7-1. Assumptions for a Hypothetical Program

Assumptions:	
Target LTI Award Value: $100,000	Annual Stock Price Growth: 15%
Stock Price: $50	Performance Period: 3 years
Black-Scholes %: 50%	Stock Price After 3 Years: $76.04

Option Grant Required:
$100,000 ÷ ($50 x 50%) = 4,000 option shares required

Performance Share Grant Required:
$100,000 ÷ $50 = 2,000 performance shares required

Performance Shares As a Percentage of Option Shares Required
2,000 ÷ 4,000 = 50%

Spectrum of Costs per Share

Figure 7-1 shows the spectrum of costs per share for an option grant. Because a competitive grant opportunity would use more shares per option, the per-share amounts do not fully expose the "relative" cost of using options under FAS 123(R). In this example, for every one performance share or restricted stock share granted, two options (4,000 × 2,000 = 2) are needed to deliver the same competitive opportunity. As a result, the spectrum of costs per competitive share is more telling of the attractiveness of performance shares in a FAS 123(R) environment (figure 7-2).

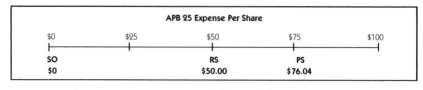

Figure 7-1. Spectrum of costs per share for an option grant

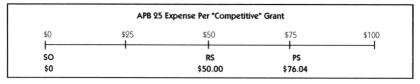

Figure 7-2. Spectrum of costs per share for a "competitive" grant of performance shares or restricted stock

How Exactly Do Performance Shares Work?

Performance shares may be defined as grants of actual shares of stock or stock units whose payment is contingent on performance as measured against pre-determined objectives over a multi-year period of time (the "cycle"); the value ultimately delivered to the participant is a function of performance against objectives *and* stock price performance during the cycle.

The key design features include (1) the term of the cycle and (2) using shares or share units. The term of the cycle is typically three to five years. I usually recommend three years in volatile businesses like high-technology industries. This recognizes the start-up nature of the plan (and long-term goal-setting process) at most businesses. It recognizes the short-term nature of planning horizon in high-technology businesses.

As for shares or versus share units, I usually recommend share units. They permit the ultimate design flexibility. Firms can choose to not credit dividends, or to credit dividends and pay currently, or to credit dividends and accumulate for payout with (and in proportion to) the earn-out of share units. Using share units also permits the extension of the relationship and restrictions beyond the termination of employment (which would not be permissible with actual shares under Internal Revenue Code Section 83); this may be desirable to enforce non-compete provisions or facilitate installment payouts after "friendly" terminations. Actual shares would require certificates to be issued (usually held by treasury), and dividends to be paid currently or accumulated during the cycle.

Predetermined Goals

Based upon my experience, I believe that a combination of an external and an internal goal best achieves most companies' objectives.

External Goal

The external goal will almost always be some form of total shareholder return (TSR) because few can argue that this measure of stock price appreciation and dividends paid is the ultimate measure of value delivered to shareholders. To dampen the impact of market vagaries on the *number of* share units ultimately earned out (their *value* will be affected by the company's stock price anyway), most companies look to relative TSR performance versus that of an index or a peer group.

Internal Goal(s)

It is often difficult to get management buy-in (or academic buy-in, for that matter) for any one financial performance measure as the "key fundamental" that trickles down to shareholder value creation consistently over time. Often, incentive plan designers find it useful to combine two competing measures in a matrix to act as checks and balances against one another, to maximize the synergistic impact of achieving both goals simultaneously, and to minimize incentive plan gamesmanship. I believe that a combination of revenue growth and operating margin goals in a matrix would reflect the still-enduring fundamental business challenge faced by any company. To the extent that revenues are growing and desired margins are achieved, by definition, cash is being managed in the shareholders' best interests if both goals are set with sufficient built-in "stretch."

Combined Goals

My preference is to combine the internal goals into one earn-out matrix, with subsequent adjustment based on performance against the external relative TSR measure, which would act as a "governor" on overall earn-outs under the plan. The external goal adjustment schedule would look like table 7-2. The internal goal matrix might look like table 7-3.

Table 7-2. External Goal Adjustment Schedule

TSR vs. Peers	% Award Adjustment
90th Percentile	150%
75th Percentile	125%
50th Percentile	100%
40th Percentile	50%
< 40th Percentile	25%

How Many Units?

Maximum Share Units

There needs to be a maximum number of units that can be earned in order to manage to the shareholder-approved limits on the plan, so I usually suggest a 200% of target award as a maximum.

Table 7-3. Internal Goal Matrix

		Cumulative Revenue vs. Plan									
		< 60%	60%	70%	80%	90%	100%	110%	120%	130%	140%
Cumulative Earning Before Tax vs. Plan	140%	0%	100%	113%	125%	138%	150%	163%	175%	188%	200%
	130%	0%	88%	100%	113%	125%	138%	150%	163%	175%	188%
	120%	0%	75%	88%	100%	113%	125%	138%	150%	163%	175%
	110%	0%	63%	75%	88%	100%	113%	125%	138%	150%	163%
	100%	0%	50%	63%	75%	88%	100%	113%	125%	138%	150%
	90%	0%	38%	50%	63%	75%	88%	100%	113%	125%	138%
	80%	0%	25%	38%	50%	63%	75%	88%	100%	113%	125%
	70%	0%	13%	25%	38%	50%	63%	75%	88%	100%	113%
	60%	0%	0%	13%	25%	38%	50%	63%	75%	88%	100%
	< 60%	0%	0%	0%	0%	0%	0%	0%	0%	0%	0%

		Cumulative Revenue vs. Plan									
		< 80%	80%	85%	90%	95%	100%	105%	110%	115%	120%
Cumulative Earning Before Tax vs. Plan	120%	$0.00	$10.00	$12.50	$15.00	$17.50	$20.00	$22.50	$25.00	$27.50	$30.00
	115%	$0.00	$8.75	$10.94	$13.13	$15.31	$17.50	$20.00	$22.50	$25.00	$27.50
	110%	$0.00	$7.50	$9.38	$11.25	$13.13	$15.00	$17.50	$20.00	$22.50	$25.00
	105%	$0.00	$6.25	$7.81	$9.38	$10.94	$12.50	$15.00	$17.50	$20.00	$22.50
	100%	$0.00	$5.00	$6.25	$7.50	$8.75	$10.00	$12.50	$15.00	$17.50	$20.00
	95%	$0.00	$3.75	$5.00	$6.25	$7.50	$8.75	$10.94	$13.13	$15.31	$17.50
	90%	$0.00	$2.50	$3.75	$5.00	$6.25	$7.50	$9.38	$11.25	$13.13	$15.00
	85%	$0.00	$1.25	$2.50	$3.75	$5.00	$6.25	$7.81	$9.38	$10.94	$12.50
	80%	$0.00	$0.00	$1.25	$2.50	$3.75	$5.00	$6.25	$7.50	$8.75	$10.00
	< 80%	$0.00	$0.00	$0.00	$0.00	$0.00	$0.00	$0.00	$0.00	$0.00	$0.00

Target Share Units

The target number of units awarded by position should be competitively driven. Theoretically, performance shares should entirely replace stock options, but they could merely be part of a "blend" of long-term incentive opportunities that still includes options (because in years of outstanding stock performance there is much more leveraged gain delivered from an option than from performance shares), and they could be carved out of the total long-term incentive "pie" from existing competitive option opportunities.

What About the Indexed Options We Hear So Much About?

A charge to earnings for stock options does open the door for adding performance bells and whistles to options that were not practical when options expensing made these added features unappealing. Options are not the best incentive, however, and adding these bells and whistles begs the question, "If we are going to be taking a charge to earnings and explaining it to shareholders via enhanced IR activities, why not use the best tool in our incentive compensation toolbox?" The vast majority of designs of performance-based options are still fully linked to the vagaries of stock market performance. Choosing an index to adjust the exercise price is fraught with potential for abuse and fraud. For example, many high-tech companies would love to have their indexed options' strike prices adjusted by relative changes in the S&P 500 index, but would it make sense or be fair? Probably not.

Performance Shares Win the Beauty Contest

Performance shares offer the best balance of objective and subjective performance measurement while substantially reducing the compensation costs, overhang, and run rate of stock compensation in a FAS 123(R) environment.

Designing Shorter-Term Cash Incentive Programs: Getting the Basics Right

Fred E. Whittlesey

Those interested in understanding stock-based compensation find themselves faced with a barrage of buzzwords describing various types of plans: stock options, employee stock ownership plans (ESOPs), employee stock purchase plans (ESPPs) . . . the list goes on. But the topic of incentive compensation, which rightly includes stock-based plans though it typically refers in practice to shorter-term cash-based programs, has its own vernacular: variable pay, lump sum awards, bonus, commission, gainsharing, profit sharing, and more. I have even seen this proliferation of terminology lead to debates over "risk sharing" versus "success sharing."

Compensation management comes down to this challenge: effective allocation of an organization's financial capital to its human capital. Every organization, whether for profit or not-for-profit, private sector or public sector, faces this challenge. In some manner and in some form—cash, stock, goods, and services—capital must be allocated to ensure people will accomplish the work of the organization.

Increasingly our human capital means more than employees; it includes other workers such as contractors, consultants, and other professional advisors, making it necessary to consider how

127

we allocate capital to the organization's *workers*, not just its employees. Developing an allocation plan requires determining who receives the capital, in what amount, based on what criteria, and then integrating this process with other management systems.

Employee ownership discussions typically revolve around the allocation of stock, but it is possible—indeed, sometimes preferable—to use cash-based programs to reinforce ownership processes, including information-sharing, empowerment, and participation. This chapter will help readers understand how to use shorter-term cash-based incentive compensation programs to reinforce ownership behaviors and create an ownership culture.

Allocating Capital: Stock-Based Plans

When we allocate financial capital to workers in the form of stock, some aspects of plan design are easy to resolve. While there are many accounting, tax, and securities law complexities, the performance measurement is usually predefined: stock price. Over time, total return to shareholders (stock price appreciation plus dividends) determines exactly how much compensation will be paid, linked directly to company performance. This inherently addresses three fundamental issues of reward strategy:

- *Performance measurement,* defined as total return to shareholders.

- *Economic consequences of performance:* in most plans, rewards are linear with increases in shareholder value.

- *Funding* provided by the marketplace (public or private) when the equity position is liquidated.

Many organizations, unable or unwilling to use actual equity for compensation, attempt to emulate a stock-based program through a long-term cash bonus plan, which often gets labeled as phantom stock or stock appreciation rights (SARs).[1] To manage an organization effectively, however, we need to focus on shorter-term measures, shorter-term behaviors, and shorter-term performance as well. We can choose stock or cash as the form of reward delivery. When we consider allocating cash or stock based on shorter-term performance (weekly, monthly, quarterly, but most commonly annually), we run into some difficult issues.

Performance Measurement

The first issue to resolve is performance measurement. If an organization embarks on an incentive compensation development process without knowing, in concept, the performance basis, the effort will be ineffective. Once we allocate stock to a worker, we know the ultimate value of that reward will be based on the stock price. The only other decisions are how many shares to allocate and what criteria will determine share allocation. But when we allocate cash it must be based on some behavior, as gauged by some measure or measures, over some period—and none of these has an inherent design answer.

For example, when the total quality management (TQM) movement began to spread widely in the early 1990s, many organizations modified their plans to reward quality, which led to failed programs and caused many to question the effectiveness of incentives. The unfortunate answer is that the wrong question was being asked. Quality is not the ultimate objective of an organization, but a strategy for meeting objectives. Clarifying objectives is the critical first step in defining performance measures as a basis for incentive compensation.

I have a simple analogy to illustrate the core issues of performance measurement (figure 8-1). Even for those who are not sports fans, this model clarifies the key issues in developing effective performance measures for shorter-term incentive programs. It contrasts the variety of performance measures in a typical business organization with those of a professional football team.

The *ultimate* objective of a for-profit entity is total shareholder return, not market share, worker satisfaction, or quality products, which are strategies. To link incentive compensation to performance measures, we must understand the types of measures are *critical* to achieving the organization's ultimate objectives. And

The Hierarchy of Performance Objectives

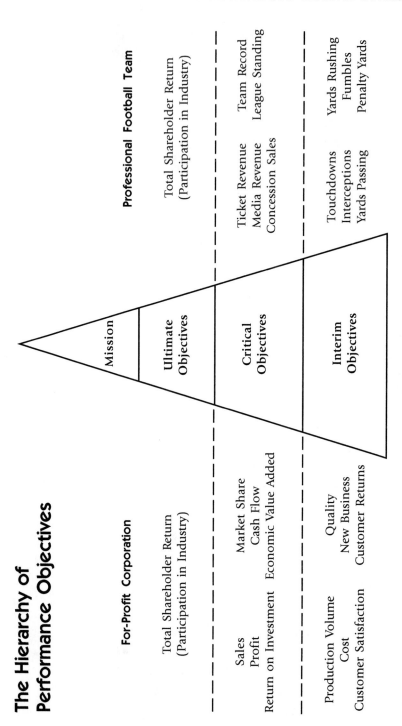

Figure 8-1. Hierarchy of performance objectives

there are many *interim* measures that contribute to higher-order measures.

Measuring Organizations and Individuals

The owners of any business, including a football team, have a dual agenda. Although they certainly want and expect a competitive return on investment, they typically direct their investment not only to a potentially profitable venture, but one in which they're interested. So they have two goals: shareholder return and industry participation. Owning a football team can be very profitable, but many wealthy investors choose instead to sponsor an auto racing team or invest in oil drilling operations to achieve their investment objectives.

But a football team owner would have little success in approaching the defensive linemen and telling them their job is to ensure a 25% return on the owner's investment. Imagine the blank stares. That is, in fact, their job, however. Sadly, this is no different than an electric utility that tells its linemen (who climb poles rather than tackle opponents) that compensation from their new stock option plan is based on increases in stock price, which depends on earnings per share (EPS) growth. In both cases, the shareholders are attempting to link rewards to the organization's ultimate objective: increasing shareholder value. And in both cases the worker is unlikely to understand how tackling quarterbacks or repairing power lines affects return on investment.

Clearly, certain measures will lead to increases in value if managed properly. But the variety and complexity of these factors may still be beyond many workers' lines of sight. The defensive tackle still may not see the connection between his performance and concession sales volume (although professional athletes are quickly catching on to the commercial appeal of their brand). But the defensive tackle's performance—continued thrashing of the other team's players—may be what generates the excitement that entices fans to attend or watch the game, thus increasing overall revenue.

When we talk about creating an ownership culture, this must be the focus. How do we get every worker to understand how he

or she affects overall performance? How do we help flight atten-
dants understand their impact on the company's stock price, then
link compensation to their behaviors accordingly? We typically
use stock as our currency when we pursue this strategy. But that
doesn't have to be the case. Many companies are unwilling, or
unable, to use stock as the primary currency for performance-
based compensation, yet succeed in creating an ownership culture.

Regardless of company size, an environment where employees feel the impact of ownership economics—upside and down-
side—is possible without the use of equity. While this chapter
will not explore the role of related processes such as information
sharing and participative management, these strategies need not
be any different for a quarterly revenue sharing plan than for a
retirement-oriented ESOP or stock option plan with a four-year
vesting schedule and ten-year term.

Designing effective shorter-term incentive programs requires
understanding and clarifying the ultimate, critical, and interim
objectives along with the responsibilities for achieving them, then
tying them to significant economic consequences for workers.

Understanding Incentive Alternatives

Management compensation plans were the source of today's performance-based cash compensation models, just as they were the
origin of equity-based compensation plans. Generally, the higher
a worker is in the management hierarchy, the more performance
measures lean toward ultimate objectives; the lower in the hierarchy, the more focus on critical or interim objectives (figure 8-
2). From a financial perspective, the question is where we "draw
the line" on the income statement. Senior management is responsible for total return on capital and is directly involved in managing both return and capital. A sales manager may have responsibility only for revenue, perhaps gross margin.

When we extend this to all workers, we have the proliferation
of buzzwords (figure 8-3) we've been subjected to over the years.
Some have emerged recently while others date back to the early

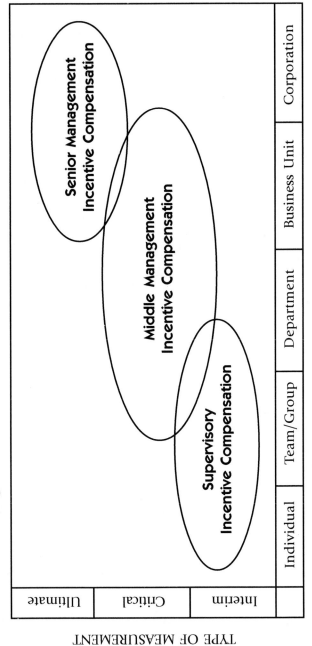

Figure 8-2. Taxonomy of short-term incentives: management

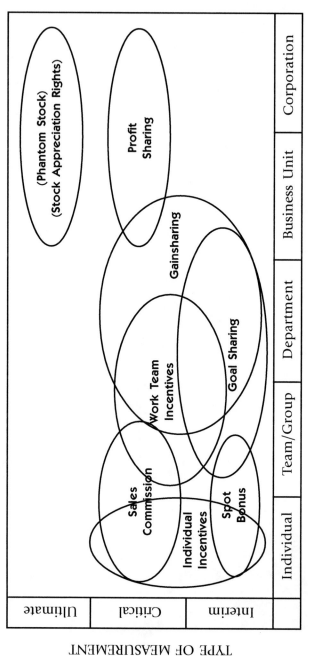

Figure 8-3. Taxonomy of short-term incentives: all workers

part of the 20th century. These result from attempts to resolve the issues of performance measures and organization levels in developing performance-based reward programs. Organizations considering performance-based cash compensation should not be intimidated by this plethora of terms. My clients' experiences show that a solid business-based process can lead through this maze of labels, and the final product—an effective performance-based pay program—can be named at the end. The key is understanding critical design decisions and the central issues of each.

Design Decisions

Many key design decisions in shorter-term cash-based incentive programs parallel those in the equity-based plan design process, not unlike the journalist's who, what, when, where, why, and how. But because we have more flexibility, the process requires more thought to arrive at the best answers, answers that address these components. Interestingly, the growing move toward equity compensation vehicles other than stock options—such as performance shares—requires companies to assess these issues as they explore alternatives to stock options.[2]

Participation. Who will participate in the plan? When we design an ESOP, there's little leeway. With a broad-based option plan, it is typically the same: all employees, sometimes even including nonemployee workers. The flexibility of shorter-term cash based programs allows a single program for everyone or just for some, or multiple programs including some or all employees. We need to determine whose behavior we are trying to change.

Performance Measures. Next, for that group or groups, what types of behavior do we seek and what outcomes do we want? What do we need them to do that they're not doing? What do we want them to stop doing? This requires defining the term *behavior* quite broadly. The first behavior a worker exhibits is responding to the company's need for workers, then interviewing, accepting the offer, and showing up the first day. The final behaviors are giving notice, winding down, leaving . . . and telling others about their employment experience after they leave.

Between the beginning and end are the behaviors we typically seek to change. But "performance" includes joining, staying, and leaving as well as actual contributions to productivity on the job. Hiring bonuses, retention bonuses, and severance packages are no less a part of shorter-term cash-based compensation strategies than profit sharing, gainsharing, and sales commissions. While these others forms of cash compensation are beyond the scope of this section, it is important to remember that these other "transitional payments" may be a significant part of total compensation and in some cases overshadow efforts to develop what we consider to be an "incentive" program.

Performance Measurement Level. At which level should we link performance? Corporate, business unit, division, department, work group, individual—or some combination? This is often the most difficult decision as we attempt to balance line of sight with team orientation, and immediate impact versus long-term impact. The lower in the organization we go and the more we move from line to staff positions, the more difficult it is to resolve these questions. The chief financial officer should be tied primarily, if not exclusively, to company financial performance. But what about the controller? assistant controller? accounts receivable clerk? There is no easy answer to these issues, but the outcome must be consistent with all other organization philosophies and strategies. "We're all in this together" or "It's everyone for themselves." "I don't have control over that" or "We all have an impact on everything."

A key decision is whether individual performance has a role in *determining* awards or *influencing* awards. This may sound like semantic nitpicking, but the former may result in an elimination of a payment while the latter may only reduce the payment by a percentage. This is often one of the design aspects creating the most heated discussions.

Performance Period. What is the relevant period for measuring performance? In most cases, a shorter-term cash incentive plan will have a performance period of one year or less. This convention in compensation design reflects the one-year horizon of the accounting cycle: annual financial statements, current versus non-current assets and liabilities, and so on. But the traditional short-term/long-term distinction is being blurred by changes occurring in equity compensation design. What about a 15-month performance measurement period followed by a 6-month vesting period? That, in fact, exactly fit one company's turnaround and product strategy timeline and was implemented successfully.

We need to provide rewards on a cycle consistent with the organization's decision-result cycle, regardless of quarterly and annual fiscal periods. One company has sales representatives on a weekly commission plan—it sells advertising in a weekly publication, and the customer must decide each week whether to advertise again. Another company has technical people working on products with a two- to three-year development cycle and a two- to three-year market life. It pays milestone awards during development and a royalty-based award after the product is released. This decision will differ most by industry and company strategy and least by company philosophy.

Performance-Award Scale. How much pay for how much performance? If we have a simple percent-of-results formula—e.g., sales reps receive a straight commission of 5% of sales—this is self-defining. But relying on a simple linear formula may yield unexpected results. In fact, in my consulting experience this is one of the most common sources of compensation disasters.[3] More often, there is a business need to ensure a minimum performance level.

It is clear that we should be willing to pay our target incentive award at our target performance level. Below that, we must decide at what level we are no longer willing to pay. This defines the "performance threshold": the level where we consider the worker to have already been fully compensated for efforts and results through base salary, benefits, and other forms of reward.

Above the target level, we must determine when we are willing to pay 10% more, 20% more, 50% more, and so on. At what

Table 8-1. Example of a Revenue and Operating Margin Matrix for an Incentive Compensation Program

Operating Cash Flow Margin%	Margin Award Factor	Percentage of Targeted Award Paid				
13.0%	130%	65%	104%	130%	143%	156%
12.0%	120%	60%	96%	120%	132%	144%
11.0%	110%	55%	88%	110%	121%	132%
10.0%	100%	50%	80%	**100%**	110%	120%
9.0%	90%	45%	72%	90%	99%	108%
8.0%	70%	35%	56%	70%	77%	84%
7.0%	50%	25%	40%	50%	55%	60%

Award Factor	**50%**	**80%**	**100%**	**110%**	**120%**

Revenue (in Millions)	**$160**	**$180**	**$200**	**$220**	**$240**
Percentage of Target	80%	90%	**Target**	110%	120%

point, if any, would we be willing to double the award? Or are we willing to continue increasing the award proportionately as performance increases, with no cap? If the plan has multiple performance measures, this scale may vary among the measures. For example, an incentive compensation program with a revenue and operating cash flow matrix may have a threshold of 80% of target for sales and 70% for operating margin (table 8-1).

This decision drives the need to conduct detailed financial modeling of any proposed incentive program before implementation.

Funding. Where will the money come from? This critical decision defines not only the plan's financial operation but also the organization's reward philosophy. Some feel an incentive opportunity should be "self funding"—that is, incentive dollars become available only when performance exceeds an expected level; this is the basis for most gainsharing plans. Others believe the incentive is part of the total cash compensation budget paid for target

Table 8-2. Sample Funding Formula

Return on Invested Capital	Percentage of Target Incentive Pool Funded
18%	130%
17%	120%
16%	110%
15%	**100%**
14%	90%
13%	70%
12%	50%
below 12%	0%

performance; this is typical of most executive incentive and other target-based plans.

A formal funding formula may ensure a certain level of organization performance occurs before incentive awards are paid, as a control to ensure individual awards, in aggregate, do not exceed the organization's ability or willingness to pay. Alternatively, we can simply set individual award targets and, through detailed financial modeling, make sure individual and organization performance levels, as defined in the plan, are well-integrated with the award structure. This is often not the case, however, and aggregate individual awards may end up above target while overall company performance is below target. This is more of a performance management issue than a compensation design issue and beyond the scope of this chapter, but it supports the need for thorough analysis of a plan's financial dynamics before implementation.

The funding method must be considered along with the performance-award scale. There may be no separate formula, or a formula may be based on a threshold, target, and maximum (table 8-2).

Allocation to Individuals. How do we determine the amount of payments to individual workers? Several alternatives are available for determining the amount. Most plans establish a target percentage of base salary and a percentage-of-salary performance-award scale, often combined with multiple performance objectives. But many still use a percentage of profit, an equal percentage of pay to all workers, or an equal dollar payment to all workers (usually only in unionized environments).

Award Payment. Once earned, when should the payment be made? Most shorter-term incentive programs pay awards soon after the performance period ends. This ensures a reasonably short period between performance and reward. The lag between performance completion and reward is typically extended only to collect and confirm the information on performance. For an annual plan, this may require completing the audited financial statements.

Regulatory Considerations

Addressing the above issues results in a blueprint for an effective shorter-term incentive program that holds all the potential of equity-based programs for creating an ownership culture. Before implementation, however, we must consider certain regulatory factors. Shorter-term cash programs are subject to substantially less regulation than stock-based programs, but several issues may render a conceptually effective plan design administratively or legally prohibitive:

- *Overtime Calculations.* The Fair Labor Standards Act and many state labor laws require inclusion of lump-sum incentive award payments in the base rate for calculating overtime.

- *Benefit Calculations.* Companies implementing new add-on plans should review all existing benefit programs to verify the definition of "compensation" and determine whether the current plan includes, or should include, incentive awards in the calculation. This may affect life and disability coverage, defined benefit and defined contribution plans, and other plans with pay-related formulas.

- *Securities Regulations.* Most cash-based incentive compensation plans with performance periods of one year or less will not be subject to securities regulations. But federal and state securities regulators are now moving toward characterizing any compensation plan based on company value as a security and are imposing certain reporting requirements.

- *ERISA.* The Employee Retirement Income Security Act of 1974, as amended, prescribes rules for any plan that may be characterized as a retirement plan. In practice, deferring payment of earned awards beyond the termination date or for more than two years may subject the plan to ERISA reporting requirements and even funding requirements.

- *Deferred Compensation Rules.* Creative attempts to structure cash incentives may inadvertently be subject to the deferred compensation rules in Internal Revenue Code Section 409A, added by the American Jobs Creation Act of 2004. Most plans will not be affected, but this is another new design "checkpoint" that must be remembered.

Implementing and Integrating the New Plan

A new incentive program must be designed with the organization's current total economic reward system in mind. The reported failure of many incentive programs can be attributed to implementing a plan with an insignificant reward opportunity relative to the existing reward structure. Employers should remember that the current group of employees has come to work for the company for, presumably, an acceptable total compensation and employment structure. An added form of compensation, if expected to change behavior, must bear some relative and absolute measure of magnitude to existing rewards.[4]

For example, a new incentive program that offers a target award of 3% of base salary is likely providing a 1% to 2% potential increase in total compensation. When compared, in the worker's mind, to the potential for a 3% merit increase, a 2% sick day bonus (five paid sick days per year), and other explicit and implicit rewards, a behavioral change is unlikely to occur. A more significant shift in total compensation may be necessary, e.g., freezing base salary for three years while adding 5% per year to the incentive pool, resulting in a more significant reward opportunity: 15% of base salary, which is then 10% below market average. This highlights the need for both "gain" and "pain" in a true ownership environment.

The first plan described above I consider an "add-on plan," where a company already offering a comprehensive compensation and benefits program offers to pay additional compensation. The latter I term a "replacement plan," where a new incentive plan substitutes for some or all of an existing form of compensation. While a replacement plan is often perceived as more controversial and requires more intensive communication, it produces more significant and rapid changes in behavior.

Joining the Performance Revolution

Surveys show that most U.S. employees now participate in one or more performance-based incentive compensation programs and have some portion of pay at risk in addition to the stale "merit increase" in base salary. I know of no organization not already using or considering performance-based cash compensation for every employee. This is occurring in publicly traded companies, closely held companies, government entities, nonprofit organizations, and companies worldwide as capitalism spreads.

U.S. employers have spent decades experimenting with incentive compensation, with much written about the successes and failures. As with any management technique, many good ideas are implemented in the wrong environment or with little thought to the details, yielding failure. But it is hard to argue with the long-term success of the U.S. economy, which is based on a combination of cash and equity-based incentives directly related to economic performance. The economic system works, and capital is allocated among organizations to its most efficient use. The same system works just as well *within* an organization, but must receive at least a fraction of the thought and effort that has led to our nation's success. We will then be able to allocate the organization's financial capital to its human capital in a way that ensures economic success for all parties.

Notes

1. Fred Whittlesey, "Expanding the Phantom Stock Concept," *Compensation and Benefits Review*, November–December 1994.

2. Fred Whirttlesey and Matt Ward, "The New Equity Compensation Map," *WorldatWork Journal*, Second Quarter 2003.

3. Fred Whittlesey and Carol Maurer, "Ten Common Compensation Mistakes," *Compensation and Benefits Review*, July–August 1993.

4. Fred Whittlesey, "Changing Employee Behavior in a Changing Workplace," *Compensation and Benefits Management*, Winter 1999.

Gainsharing and the Scanlon Plan

Paul W. Davis

Today there is increased interest in gainsharing, a management concept that has endured for over half a century. Gainsharing is a guiding management philosophy of at least 5 of the "100 Best Companies to Work for in America": Herman Miller, Donnelly, Beth Israel Hospital, Motorola, and Dana all credit at least part of their world-class performance to their gainsharing systems.[1] A comprehensive study conducted by the American Compensation Association beginning in 1991 and published in 1994 found that companies averaged over $2,410 per employee per year in productivity and quality improvements after installing gainsharing. After deducting program expenses and paying bonuses on average of $867 per employee per year, gainsharing provided a 134% return.[2] The financial results are impressive, yet they are only one of the many benefits of gainsharing. Study after study has found that gainsharing also improves employee involvement, communication, teamwork, labor relations, and quality.[3]

The renewed interest in such an old concept can be attributed to pressures that organizations are now facing. As they downsize, they seek ways to motivate the remaining employees. As they become flatter, the old methods of compensation (number of direct reports, etc.) are no longer effective. As competitive pressures increase, they seek ways to increase productivity and quality. After adopting Total Quality Management (TQM) practices, they seek ways to reward and coordinate teams. Unable to afford the high cost of adversarial relationships and ever-increasing base wages, union and management leaders look to gainsharing as a way to encourage cooperation within collective bargaining.

What Is Gainsharing?

The Japanese have a fable about a crow and a cormorant. In this ancient tale, a crow admires the cormorant, a black water bird that can swim to catch fish. The crow reasons that because he is a black bird like the cormorant, he too should be able to swim, so he dives into the water, only to drown. The fable's lesson is that things that appear to be the same may not, due to subtle, unapparent differences. Those interested in gainsharing should remember the crow's experience, because gainsharing systems that at first appear to be identical reveal fundamental differences upon closer scrutiny.

Gainsharing is a generic term with widely different definitions. For many, gainsharing is simply a group bonus calculation. For others, gainsharing describes a very sophisticated organizational development strategy. For the purpose of this chapter, gainsharing will describe any organizational process designed to increase productivity, quality, and financial performance by sharing "rewards" with groups of employees. Furthermore, in this chapter gainsharing will refer to practices that include (1) establishing specific goals, targets, or baselines; (2) communicating these goals, targets, or baselines to a group of employees; and (3) sharing rewards when the goals, targets, or baselines are exceeded.

This operational definition of gainsharing will not include discretionary management "bonus" practices such as an annual Christmas bonus because they are not tied to the specific performance of the company. In addition, it will not include individual piecework systems because they reward individuals and not groups. However, profit sharing will be considered a form of "gainsharing."

The ABCs of Gainsharing

Most of what is written about gainsharing concerns the mechanics of bonus formulas because various gainsharing systems are typically classified by how the bonus formula is constructed. In these articles, Scanlon Plans, Multicost Scanlon Plans, Rucker Plans®, Improshare®, Profit Sharing, etc., are reduced to a paragraph that only an accountant could love. While the formula is important for gainsharing success, it is only one factor among many that differentiate the various approaches. Recent research indicates that bonus formulas may not be the most important factors in gainsharing success.[4] Furthermore, almost all articles written since the 1960s about the Scanlon Plan's bonus calculation are misleading in documenting Scanlon evolution. They have not kept up with current Scanlon theory or application. While they are valuable as history, they provide little insight for those interested in the current state of the art in gainsharing.

The final reason why the formula approach to describing gainsharing is no longer effective is because it describes fewer and fewer gainsharing applications. Historically, gainsharing plans were one-size-fits-all packages, developed by consultants who trademarked their approaches. Improshare® and Rucker® are two of the most well known. While Improshare® Plans are still being installed, the Rucker® Plan did not survive long after the death of its creator. Today, there are still consultants trying to trademark their approaches, but most gainsharing systems are customized to the unique needs of each organization.

A new method of classifying the various gainsharing approaches is needed if the reader truly wants to understand the critical differences and make an informed choice. This chapter will attempt to help the reader understand the ABCs of gainsharing. This simple device, in which A stands for Assumptions, B for Business literacy, and C for Commitment, will help readers understand which gainsharing approach is right for them. If the ABCs can be mastered, the rest of gainsharing (including designing the bonus formula) will be easier. Because there are only two classic approaches that have survived the test of time, Scanlon and

Improshare®, they will be used to highlight differences in philosophy and application.

The "A" of the ABCs: Assumptions

All gainsharing systems are developed for some desired end. Typically, the motivation is to produce greater profits, to produce higher quality goods or services, or to encourage labor-management cooperation. At the heart of every gainsharing system are assumptions about human motivation and behavior at work. Gainsharing systems take on specific characteristics based on the assumptions of those that lead, design, and operate them. These assumptions define the program to a much greater extent than does the method of bonus calculation.

The "B" of the ABCs: Business Literacy

All gainsharing systems claim to increase productivity, profits, or performance. Some are based on the idea that the only thing needed to generate these improvements is more financial motivation, while others stress the importance of teaching employees about the business so that they will know what to improve and how to participate in improving it.

The "C" of the ABCs: Commitment

Gainsharing is a way to change the commitment level of people at work. All gainsharing systems attempt to shift commitment from the individual to a group or organization. The various approaches differ in the size of the group and the level of commitment they attempt to create.

Assumptions About Human Motivation

Throughout human history, we have sought to harness and control human motivation. We have used a wide range of "motivators" to get people to do what we want. We have used punishment from slavery to starvation, and we have used rewards from concubines to precious metals. As society became more civilized, we developed money as the universal form of exchange. With industrialization, we developed a wage system in which people work for money that they can then use to purchase desired goods and services. Despite thousands of years of experimentation, there is still great disagreement about what does and does not motivate. Because motivation is the primary reason organizations install gainsharing, the debate is not academic. Research has produced results that at times seem to contradict what most of us assume is common sense. For example, we have learned through research that money may not be as powerful a motivator as non-monetary rewards. Psychologists have attempted to unravel the mystery of human motivation, yet there are still wide differences of opinion on (1) whether one human being can motivate another—is motivation intrinsic or extrinsic? (2) what motivates people at work; (3) what the best way is for managers to motivate workers; and (4) whether money is the universal motivator.

Can One Human Being Motivate Another?

All gainsharing systems use some form of incentive or financial reward. So, like the crow in the Japanese parable above, we might assume that all gainsharing philosophies believe deeply in the power of extrinsic motivation. They do not. Scanlon Plans place more of an emphasis on the intrinsic motivation created by participation and education than on the extrinsic motivation created by money. Improshare® Plans place more of an emphasis on extrinsic motivation. Alfie Kohn, author of *Punished by Rewards: The Trouble with Gold Stars Incentive Plans, A's, Praise, and Other Bribes*, argues that the only thing accomplished when we try to motivate others is to destroy the intrinsic motivation in each of us. He quotes one of the foremost management scholars and researchers on human motivation, Frederick Herzberg, who wrote:

> Managers do not motivate employees by giving them higher wages, more benefits or new status symbols. Rather, employees are motivated by their

own inherent need to succeed at a challenging task. The manager's job then, is not to motivate people to get them to achieve; instead, the manager should provide opportunities for people to achieve so they will become motivated.[5]

Herzberg said this about the typical manager's common-sense approach to motivation:

Managements have always looked at man as an animal to be manipulated with a carrot and a stick. They found that when a man hurts, he will move to avoid pain—and they say, "We're motivating the employees." Hell, you're not motivating them, you're moving them.[6]

What Motivates People at Work?

Researchers and management scholars believe that we each have different needs and, therefore, different motivators. Abraham Maslow stated that human beings fulfill their needs in a certain order. First, they have a need to eat, sleep, and breathe. He called these physiological needs. When these needs are met, he predicted, people would seek to have their security and safety needs met. Maslow believed physiological, security, and safety needs are lower-order needs. When these needs are met, people seek to have their social or affiliation needs met. Next they strive to have their esteem or ego needs met. When all the other needs are met, people seek self-actualization or self-fulfillment. Maslow believed social needs, esteem needs, and self-actualization needs are higher-order needs. Lower-order needs have more to do with our bodies; higher-order needs are related more to our minds.

Frederick Herzberg's work on motivation found that what motivates people is different from what turns them off. He found that working conditions, salary, benefits, status, and security were not motivators. He called them "hygiene factors" and realized they were similar to Maslow's lower-order needs. While they have the capacity to turn people off, they have little capacity to turn people on. Hygiene factors are a base from which the higher-order needs can be addressed. The "motivators" he discovered were responsibility, achievement, recognition, and satisfaction in the work itself. These, he realized, were related to Maslow's higher-order needs.

Herzberg's research indicates that if we want to motivate workers, we must first make sure that we have a base to work from. We must create security by driving out fear, providing insurance, and so forth. We must provide an adequate salary so the need for food and shelter can be met. Once this base is in place, we can help to provide "motivators" by creating organizations that allow the higher-order needs for affiliation, esteem, responsibility, recognition, and self fulfillment to be met.

Managers who accept Herzberg's research would create as part of any gainsharing approach opportunities for employees to have their social needs met (perhaps by having them work in teams). They would design their gainsharing system to encourage responsibility and recognition. They would make sure that everyone had a chance for meaningful achievement at work. They would be careful not to use gainsharing to create greater insecurity (by putting pay at risk). They would not view money as a motivator.

What Can Managers Do to Motivate?

As researchers have explored human motivation at work, they have also studied and written about the nature of management, trying to discover what a manager should or should not do to increase the motivation of the work force. Managers' assumptions about the nature of people at work have a tremendous effect on how they attempt to motivate others. For example, one organization that was exploring gainsharing decided not to pursue the idea further when the president of the organization said, "I do not believe in gainsharing. I grew up in the Depression. Having a job is the only gain anyone needs." He assumed that his work force shared his views. He believed that their need for security would produce motivation. He clung to his assumptions, even though most of his work force was younger and had never experienced the Great Depression. He clung to his assumptions even though they were not supported by Herzberg's research.

Managers' assumptions are also influenced by the predominant management gurus of their time. As this chapter is being written, management thought is dominated by the work of W. Edwards Deming, Tom Peters, and Stephen Covey. These writers stress the importance of employee involvement and participatory management. However, many of today's practicing managers were influenced by other writers and other philosophies that do not place a value on employee involvement and participation. Their philosophies are in conflict with current management thought. Frequently, they rely on punishment and rewards as the primary motivators at work.

There are those who still follow the theories of Frederick Taylor, one of the earliest and most influential writers about the role of management. Some even credit Taylor with coining the term "gainsharing." His book, *The Principles of Scientific Management*, written in the early 1900s, influenced a generation of managers and launched industrial engineering as a profession. The book explains how to use the principles of scientific management to motivate a steelworker to work harder by offering him more money for loading pig iron. He illustrates with an actual quote from a conversation he had with the steelworker.

> You will do exactly as this man (manager) tells you tomorrow, from morning till night. When he tells you to pick up a pig and walk, you pick it up and you walk, and when he tells you to sit down and rest, you sit down. You do that straight through the day. And what's more no backtalk. Now a high-priced man does just what he is told to do and no backtalk. Do you understand that? When the man tells you to walk, you walk, when he tells you to sit down, you sit down, and you don't talk back to him.[7]

Scientific management assumes that some people in an organization are better at thinking while others should simply do what they are told (without talking back). Money and punishment are seen as the most powerful motivators. Workers are viewed as lazy and unwilling to do their best without management intervention. It is assumed that the average worker does not seek more responsibility and in fact will avoid responsibility. Douglas McGregor, the great scholar of organizations many years later, would call these assumptions "Theory X."

Management assumptions are critical to gainsharing success. Assumptions are like lenses in a pair of glasses. They will distort, focus, and alter everything a manager sees. For example, a small Michigan manufacturing company was purchased by a group of investors who had experience with the Scanlon gainsharing system. The investors specialized in turnaround situations. The investors' assumptions about management were not "Theory X." The gainsharing approach they selected was highly participatory and involved the union and the employees in solving company problems. Within three years the company was highly profitable, having carved out a niche by competing head-to-head with the much larger 3M Corporation. The company became so successful that the investors decided to sell, receiving a tenfold return on their investment. The Theory X purchasers did not believe in the value of participatory management. Their assumptions distorted their view of the gainsharing system. They saw the bonuses as giving away some of their profits and saw the frequent meetings required for participation as a waste of time and a loss of their management power. Within two years, the gainsharing system was in ruins, employee morale was at an all-time low, and the new owners were debating moving the plant south to avoid their union.

Today, "Taylorism" has fallen out of favor, but its basic assumptions continue to drive many management actions. Theory X managers usually do not support gainsharing if there is an employee involvement component, yet they may embrace gainsharing as a compensation approach. They tend to support gainsharing systems where pay is at risk. In these systems employees are not paid a market wage, but are able to reach or surpass market rates with the addition of a gainsharing bonus. These assumptions are the same assumptions that drove Taylor's piecework systems in the early 1900s. The assumptions driving these systems are that people do not want to work, that money is the primary motivator, that employees will not work hard unless their paychecks are at risk, and that management must intervene by designing a more effective carrot if workers are to be motivated to work.

While McGregor studied managers with Theory X assumptions, he also studied managers with the opposite assumptions about people. McGregor called these assumptions "Theory Y." These managers assume that workers want to accept more responsibility, actually enjoy work, want to set their own goals, have great ambition, and can be trusted. Today, most modern management practices such as TQM, teams, employee involvement, etc., are based on Theory Y assumptions. Few managers realize that McGregor developed Theory Y by studying a variety of organizations with Scanlon gainsharing systems. McGregor endorsed Scanlon by saying, "I need only mention the Scanlon (gainsharing) Plan as the outstanding embodiment of these ideas in practice." Herman Miller, a Michigan office furniture manufacturer, has had a Scanlon gainsharing system since the 1950s. Consistently ranked as one of America's most admired corporations, the company has been a leader in Theory Y management practices. Former CEO Hugh De Pree describes the essence of Theory Y management: "The difference at Herman Miller is not the lengthened shadow of one man nor the talents of an elite group of managers. The difference is the energy beamed from thousands of unique contributions by people who understand, accept, and are committed to the idea they can make a difference."[8]

Is Money the Universal Motivator?

The assumptions behind the Scanlon gainsharing system are congruent with the work of McGregor, Maslow, and Herzberg. Scanlon systems are based on the assumption that people want to participate and accept responsibility. Other gainsharing systems were developed based on different assumptions about human motivation. Mitchell Fein, the creator of the Improshare® gainsharing system, wrote: "Herzberg's postulation that money is not a motivator, that the work itself motivates, was sweet music to managers' ears. Not only did workers not accept these notions; neither did management."[9]

Fein assumes that money is the primary motivator. While Improshare® encourages employee involvement, it is not viewed as the critical component that it is in Scanlon gainsharing systems. Fein cites his own studies, which indicate the Improshare® system motivates and creates greater productivity without the need for employee involvement. The debate has taken on renewed vigor as a result of the work of the late W. Edwards Deming. Deming, the great quality expert, had very strong feelings about motivation and the role of money as a motivator. He believed in the power of intrinsic motivation. He believed that individual merit pay systems, rewards, punishment, and most of the other motivators used in business were dysfunctional. He believed in Theory Y management. Deming summed up over 50 years of organizational study by saying, "Pay is not a motivator."

If pay is not a motivator, why is it so common? Voltaire said, "When it is a question of money, everybody is of the same religion." Leavitt writes: "Money incentives have come to occupy a central place because money is a common means for satisfying all sorts of diverse needs in our society and because money may be handled and measured. Money is 'real'; it is communicable. Many other means to need-satisfaction are abstract and ephemeral."[10]

Jerry McAdams in *The Reward Plan Advantage* takes a pragmatic approach that seeks the middle ground.[11] He does not take the extreme position of Deming or Kohn that all motivation is intrinsic, nor does he endorse the assumptions of Leavitt and Fein that extrinsic monetary rewards are sufficient motivators alone. He believes that a properly designed reward system will avoid the problems of both extremes. McAdams' credibility is enhanced by the fact that he was the head researcher in several large-scale studies of alternative reward systems for the American Compensation Association.

Because money is universal, quick, and easy, it often becomes the only focus of gainsharing systems. Gainsharing as compensation or a "bonus" is easier to design, communicate, and administer than is a more comprehensive method such as Scanlon. Scanlon practitioners have found that the real value of financial rewards is not the money they provide per se, but rather the way in which the money helps to focus employees and management on business issues. In fact, Scanlon practitioners no longer view Scanlon as simple gainsharing, as a plan, or as a program. They consider Scanlon to be a *process* for organizational and individual development. Each part of the process is important for success. Scanlon practitioners believe that most gainsharing systems have fatal flaws built into them. Typical gainsharing approaches that consider money to be the only motivator can motivate only when there are bonuses to be paid. They do not provide motivation during tough times, when a company cannot pay bonuses but needs motivated employees the most. Many operate like a lottery. Employees enjoy the opportunity to earn extra money but believe the bonus is subject to change. They do not believe they can influence the results. Their focus on gainsharing as a program or a plan, instead of a *process or system,* prevents them from adapting and changing, which creates built-in obsolescence.

There appears to be a basic paradox among gainsharing practitioners. Gainsharing is viewed as a solution for motivating workers by managers with totally opposite assumptions about what motivates workers. Each camp has its own management theorists to justify its assumptions. Each is able to cite objective studies to validate its position. Gainsharing systems are not created equal. Those exploring gainsharing must first determine their own basic assumptions about human motivation and then design a gainsharing process based on those assumptions. If they work with an existing gainsharing process or gainsharing consultant, they must question whether the process or the consultant share their assumptions.

When management assumptions and gainsharing systems match, there is power, synergy, and integrity. Gainsharing becomes a way for the manager to manage. When management assumptions and gainsharing do not match, gainsharing is not effective. Gainsharing sends a strong message to the organization about what behaviors are important. Employees are quick to find inconsistencies between what the managers say and what gainsharing rewards. While this is not to say that consistency per se makes gainsharing successful, inconsistencies will soon undermine even the best gainsharing process.

Explore Your Options

The following questions and suggestions are designed to help you explore your assumptions and determine what gainsharing approach is congruent with your assumptions. Because Scanlon and Improshare® are the only classic approaches still being installed, they are highlighted. If the reader is evaluating another approach or designing a generic gainsharing process, use the questions to help clarify your thinking.

A (Assumptions)

When evaluating your options, consider the following questions:

Do you believe workers are motivated more by extrinsic rewards or intrinsic rewards?

- If extrinsic, design a gainsharing process that focuses on money as a motivator. Consider Improshare®.

- If intrinsic, maybe you should not even consider gainsharing. If you do, consider a process that takes into consideration intrinsic motivators like participation. Consider Scanlon.

Do you agree with Herzberg that the human motivators are responsibility, achievement, recognition, and satisfaction with the work itself?

- If yes, build your plan to include these motivators. Consider Scanlon.

- If no, what do you believe are the needs of your work force? If you believe money is a universal need, design a process with a large bonus component. Consider Improshare®.

Do you believe in Theory X or Theory Y management?

- If X, consider scientific management. Consider designing a piecework system instead of gainsharing. Consider automation or contracting out as a way to increase productivity and quality. Consider putting a large part of your employees' wages at risk. Consider a merit system instead of a gainsharing system.

- If Y, involve your employees in designing the process. Do not use money as the only source of motivation. Use gainsharing to build participation and commitment. Include all employees in the gainsharing pool. Consider Scanlon.

B (Business Literacy)

One of the hottest management ideas of the late 1990s is the idea of business literacy, or "open-book management." Authors such as John Case, Jack Stack, and John Schuster have done a wonderful job of documenting the effects literacy training has had on a wide variety of organizations. Stack's own organization, Springfield ReManufacturing Corporation, has become one of the most sought-after places for a benchmark visit because of its amazing turnaround story.

What these open-book managers and authors have discovered is the power generated when employees know their business, are provided meaningful information on the performance of their business, are able to influence decisions to improve their business, and are included in the rewards of capitalism. Open-book practitioners seek to create companies where every employee is a business person.

Despite the hype, these ideas are not new. Many were developed over half a century ago by Joseph Scanlon, the father of gainsharing, and are incorporated in every Scanlon gainsharing process. Scanlon was an eclectic man. During his lifetime he was a steelworker, union leader, cost accountant, prizefighter, researcher, and lecturer at the Massachusetts Institute of Technology (MIT). His name has become synonymous with gainsharing.

During the Depression, Scanlon learned the value of cooperation by helping unemployed steelworkers find land and seed for gardens. After the Depression, he found himself on the union bargaining committee in negotiations with his employer, Empire Sheet and Tube. Barely profitable, Empire was not able to increase wages and was in danger of going under. In desperation, Scanlon sought advice from the International Brotherhood of Steelworkers. He was told to return to Empire to see if there was any way the workers could improve the company in hope of making it more profitable. The workers had many ideas for improving the company, and Empire was saved. News of Scanlon's work spread, and soon he was helping other workers and their companies cooperate to survive.

The initial Scanlon Plans had no "gainsharing" bonus formula. They focused on business literacy and employee involvement. As companies became stronger and survival was no longer the issue, the idea of sharing gains was born. The initial gainsharing formulas were designed to share improvements in labor productivity. As workers were able to reduce the cost of labor, these savings were split, with 25% of the savings going to the company and 75% going to the workers. The plans were very successful. Scanlon was asked to join the Steelworkers Research Department.

With the outbreak of World War II, Scanlon became involved in creating joint union and management councils to help with the war effort. After the war, labor and management were no longer interested in cooperation. Scanlon was asked by Douglas McGregor to join the faculty of MIT, where he was involved in establishing gainsharing systems until his death in 1956. Russell Davenport reported on the philosophy, methods, and potential of Scanlon's ideas in "The Greatest Opportunity on Earth" and "Enterprise for Everyman," two *Fortune* magazine articles in 1949 and 1950.[12] Scanlon's work was continued by Carl Frost and Fred Lesieur. Frost contributed to Scanlon theory and practice by creating the Frost/ Scanlon principles. Lesieur worked with MIT and specialized in installing Scanlon Plans in companies with unions.

The Scanlon process has survived for over half a century, and many of America's "best" organizations use Scanlon. Motorola, Herman Miller, Dana, Donnelly, Sears, Magna Copper, Beth Israel Hospital, and Whirlpool are just a few of the organizations that were influenced by Scanlon's ideas. Scanlon never trademarked his process or copyrighted his ideas, believing they should be made freely available. Today, many generic plans (and some trademarked plans) are really Scanlon Plans. Scanlon Plans are a combination of philosophy (Theory Y), principles, and common-sense practices.

Reflecting his basic belief in business literacy and employee involvement, Scanlon wrote:

> What we are trying to say is simply this: That the average worker knows his own job better than anyone else, and that there are a great many things that he could do if he has a complete understanding of the necessary. Given this opportunity of expressing his intelligence and ingenuity, he becomes a more useful and more valuable citizen in any given community or in any industrial operation.[13]

The primary Scanlon principle is called Identity. The principle of Identity incorporates what writers are today calling business literacy. Through a process of education, all employees are taught about their company, their competitors, and the need to change. Each Scanlon company develops its own process to insure Identity. Visits by customers, information on competitors, and training on how to read financial reports are all ways that Scanlon companies create Identity. Beth Israel Hospital implements Identity by sharing hospital information with its employees in three languages (French, Spanish, and English). Sears creates Identity by having employees complete "learning maps," customized colorful interactive visuals that teach employees "What Day It Is on Retail Street," "The Voices of Our Customers," and "The Sears Money Flow." Each company designs an Identity process that fits its industry and size.

When evaluating your options, consider the following questions:

Do you believe that business literacy among all employees in your company or organization is important?

- If yes, consider developing a gainsharing process that stresses the importance of business literacy. This can be done through training, but also through systems that encourage business literacy, e.g., screening committees or Great Game of Business® financial reporting systems. Include developing business literacy as part of the installation strategy of your gainsharing process. Consider Scanlon.

- If no, focus your system on the financial reward potential of gainsharing. Consider Improshare®.

Are you willing to share financial and operational data with your employees?

- If yes, read the open-book management literature for ideas on how to do this. Consider Scanlon.
- If no, business literacy is not for you! Scanlon is not for you.

C (Commitment)

Organizations are changing their commitments to customers, investors, and employees. The quality movement has helped world-class organizations increase their commitment to customers. Investors, led by large institutions, have demanded and received increased commitment to their needs. Paradoxically, during these times of increased commitment to customers and investors, organizations are decreasing their commitment to employees. Many employees work part-time, their organizations unable or unwilling to commit to full-time employment. Full-time employees are told it is impossible for their organizations to commit to lifetime employment. Organizations that have become flatter and leaner cannot even commit to regular advancement for good performers.

While employees are told to expect less organizational commitment, they are asked to commit to new forms of work. They are asked to commit to longer hours and more responsibility. They are expected to commit to being flexible. They are told to commit to lifetime learning to master ever-more complex and changing jobs.

Albert Camus said, "Commitment is the soul of work." Johann Goethe said, "Until one is committed, there is hesitancy, the chance to draw back, always ineffectiveness, concerning all acts of initiative (and creation). There is one elementary truth the ignorance of which kills countless ideas and splendid plans: That the moment one definitely commits oneself, then providence moves too."

The various gainsharing approaches differ in the commitment they make and the commitment they seek. Those that are implemented as a compensation strategy commit to pay a bonus when certain performance targets are met. This in and of itself is a major commitment, just like a commitment to meet payroll or to fund benefits. Once an organization commits to gainsharing, it must follow through with the commitment. A bonus cannot be promised and then withdrawn later. Most gainsharing systems are self-funding, paying for their administration and the bonuses out of gains or savings, yet even these systems demand organizational commitment. For example, Lincoln Electric had to borrow money to meet bonus commitments. Its system paid a bonus based on productivity gains. Employees improved productivity, yet the company was not profitable. This does not happen often, but if it does illustrate the point that a commitment to a bonus is a commitment that must be honored in good times and bad.

Gainsharing systems such as Scanlon that are fundamentally organizational and individual development systems demand great commitment from employees and their organizations. They demand personal and organizational commitment to participation, to fairness, and to increased competency.

Gainsharing and Commitment

Commitment to Participation

Every gainsharing system seeks to alter the commitment of individuals. As a result of gainsharing, individuals are assumed to participate in some way to making the group or organization better. The various approaches differ on how widely to encourage participation and on who is included in the gainsharing group. Some focus only on the production people in an organization and do not include administrative staff or managers. Some focus on teams, with each team operating its own bonus system. Some focus on multiple plants or sites. Gainsharing writers call this the "line of sight" issue. People want to be able to influence the results of a bonus. The more people that are involved, the more difficult this becomes. The less a bonus measure is influenced by participation, the harder it is to explain and to enlist support. For example, employees in a manufacturing operation might feel that they can participate in reducing scrap; yet they may feel they have no control over profits, even though the two measures are related.

The question of who to include in the gainsharing group becomes a question of philosophy and pragmatism. The Scanlon philosophy is to include as many as possible. Thus all levels and jobs are usually identified as participants. This creates a "we are all in it together" state of mind. It makes it easier for departments and teams to work together because they share the same Scanlon bonus. It allows white- and blue-collar workers to find common ground. In large organizations such as Sears (with over 300,000 employees), the group has been defined as a specific store or store support service unit. This fits Sears' organizational structure and allows for a manageable size. In smaller organizations, the group may be defined as the entire organization. Sometimes even part-time employees and key vendors are included in the process.

Commitment to participation can be built into gainsharing or it can be left to chance. For example, historically the Scanlon approach encourages participation through a suggestion system and committee structure. Employees submit suggestions to a production committee made up of coworkers and managers who decide whether to implement the suggestions. Production committees are workgroup- or department-based. Production committees send representatives to a screening committee made up of top management and union leaders. The screening committee reviews suggestions that were rejected and those suggestions that involve multiple departments or large expenditures of money to implement. This system exists in many organizations as well as some newer forms of participation such as work teams and Kaizan teams.

Employees in Scanlon companies are expected to participate by "influencing decisions in their areas of competence." The commitment to participation is evident in the way the Scanlon process is implemented. Scanlon Plans are not purchased off-the-shelf from consultants or third parties. They are not implemented unless there is evidence of virtually universal organizational commitment at all levels. The process begins with discussions at the top level of the organization. Every top leader, after learning about the Scanlon process, is asked to make a personal and professional commitment of support. Only when the top-level team is personally and professionally committed is the Scanlon process introduced to the other levels of the organization. If there is a union, the union leadership is introduced to the idea. Eventually all levels of management, including the front-line supervisors, are introduced to the concepts of Scanlon and asked to make a personal and professional commitment of support. When the managers representing the organization, their departments, and their professions have committed and the union leadership has committed, the process is explained to the rank-and-file employees. They too are asked to commit to creating a different way of working through the Scanlon process. They vote to participate by electing a committee to design the Scanlon system. After it is designed, the committee presents its work to all of the employees, and a vote to try Scanlon for a trial period is taken. Acceptance levels of 80-90% are usually required for the process to be implemented. Finally, after the trial period, the Scanlon process is evaluated one more time and a vote is taken to continue Scanlon indefinitely as a way of working together.

This process is time-consuming. It takes an average of 35 weeks from initial exploration until Scanlon is approved for the trial period. The process is designed not for speed but rather for building commitment and participation. The result is:

- The process builds commitment: People "own" the Scanlon process, even giving it a unique name such as UNITE, PRIDE, REACH, or I.C.E.

- The process does not belong to one department, e.g., Human Resources.

- The process prevents Scanlon from becoming another "flavor of the month" approach.

- The process requires an organization to spend time up front explaining gainsharing rather than risking that people will understand later once it is in place.

- The process prevents one-size-fits-all mistakes because each company is treated as the unique entity it is.

- The process builds internal competence. A company does not become dependent on consultants or others to maintain or improve the system. Employees grow as human beings as they learn new skills.

- The process creates the links and support needed for implementation as well as design.

- The process creates a model that can be used when it needs to be renewed.

- The process leads to success: a study done at the University of Wisconsin found that participation, voting, and plan understanding were highly correlated with gainsharing success.[14]

The idea of employee voting is intimidating to some, especially with an 80–90% approval rate recommended. However, the vote rarely fails. More typically, as the Scanlon process unfolds, issues will surface that may require a delay or change in the process. For example, one company decided not to pursue Scanlon because it was involved in ISO certification and the top managers did not feel they could handle both initiatives at the same time. Once ISO was completed, the company began the Scanlon process. Others may decide not to continue because the union will not support gainsharing or the top management team cannot accept Theory Y management practices. The commitment level the process generates is illustrated by what happened in a recent Sears installation. A long-term employee became sick and was taken to the hospital on the day the vote was to be taken. She called from her hospital bed because she wanted the vote to be unanimous.

Other gainsharing approaches require little commitment to participate from employees. They are designed by internal or external consultants and then simply communicated to employees. They can be installed quickly. There is no vote. They can be changed quickly and easily. They do not create commitment.

The issues surrounding participation and gainsharing are similar to the issues surrounding participation and employee stock ownership. Participation is not required for gainsharing nor is it required for ownership. Participation is linked to the strategy or reason for adopting gainsharing as it is linked to the reasons for adopting ESOPs. Some gainsharing systems are viewed as a compensation strategy, and participation is not required. Some ESOPs are viewed as a tax-saving strategy, and participation is not required. Research on both gainsharing and employee stock ownership have found that effectiveness is increased when combined with participation.

When evaluating your options, consider the following questions:

Do you wish to commit to participation?

- If yes, consider designing participation into the system from the beginning by having employees create the system. Make sure top leadership is committed to making gainsharing a success. Consider Scanlon.

- If no, Improshare® may still require more participation than you feel comfortable with. Do *not* consider Scanlon.

Do you have time for participation?

- If yes, consider a process like Scanlon.

- If no, wait until you have time. You simply cannot have meaningful participation if you do not take the time.

Commitment to Equity (Fairness)

Scanlon gainsharing systems define equity (in the sense of fairness and impartiality, not an ownership interest) as a genuine commitment to accounting for the needs of all constituents, including customers, investors, and employees. The pursuit of equity is the way the Scanlon gainsharing system holds everyone accountable to the stakeholders. Scanlon is the only gainsharing process that defines these multiple accountabilities, yet the idea is probably as old as time itself. Confucius was reported to have said, "The proper man understands equity, the small man profits." Equity is important because a focus on only one or two of the stakeholders will ultimately destroy an organization. For example, the auto industry in the U.S. historically has been a good place to work, with high pay and good benefits. It has also been a good place to invest, yet consumers began switching en masse to Japanese automobiles in the 1970s because they were not happy with the quality and service of U.S. companies. The U.S. was close to losing the industry until the auto companies and their employees made the gut-wrenching changes needed to compete. There are companies whose profitability is unacceptably low or nonexistent, yet whose employees demand higher and higher wages, eventually forcing the company to go out of business. Today, there are companies that lay off their employees even though they are highly profitable, with record sales. Such companies are liquidating their human assets and setting in motion their own demise.

Carl Frost, in describing the Scanlon equity process, wrote:

> During the early days of Scanlon and somewhat persistently since, many have defined equity as bonuses. The early days were adversarial. Wages were not nationally uniform or substantial. Too often management permitted and even encouraged the expectation of supplemental income, primarily as a result of productivity improvements, i.e., Improshare®, gainsharing. The use of the word share often suggests difference and division rather than neutrality of benefits that are mutually inclusive rather than exclusive.[15]

Scanlon companies operationalize the equity concept by creating appropriate reliable databases of customer satisfaction, financial performance, and human resources. There are regular, public occasions where the data are shared and discrepancies between what is and what needs to be are explored. Sometimes positive discrepancies are noted, and sometimes negative discrepancies are found. Frequently, bonus formulas are constructed that take into account the needs of all stakeholders. Sears has developed a "Total Performance Index" as a component of corporate transformation. The vision is to make Sears a compelling place to shop, to work, and to invest. Customer, employee, and investor measures are tracked. Spring Engineering and Manufacturing Company even named their Scanlon system the I.C.E. (Investor, Customer, and Employee) Plan to emphasize equity. The Scanlon Equity Principle includes many concepts business writers are now calling a "balanced scorecard."

Bonus formulas that take into account the needs of all stakeholders are better than those that emphasize only one. The Lincoln Electric bonus, mentioned earlier, might satisfy employees but may not meet the needs of investors. One company paid a bonus to employees for improvement in quality, yet the firm's customers said the company's quality standards were too low. The company found itself rewarding employees for performance that its customers would not accept. These examples illustrate the difficulty in creating equity. It is much easier to simply create a bonus. However, an equity system is superior to a bonus system alone because equity provides the greatest long-term organizational security. Those involved in Scanlon gainsharing find that the primary reason employees are interested in developing a Scanlon process is to provide long-term employment security and not to provide short-term bonuses.

Companies that stress a bonus create employees who are dissatisfied when the bonus cannot be paid. These employees are conditioned to expect a bonus. They are not aware that their investors may be losing money or that their customers have gone somewhere else. In companies committed to equity, employees know the needs of the other stakeholders and are willing to make sacrifices when necessary.

Organizations operationalize the principle of equity in many ways. Traditionally, they decide what to measure and then construct a historical baseline that represents the current level of the measure(s). When the measure(s) is exceeded, the gain is split between the company and the employees. Operational measures such as labor productivity, scrap, safety, or quality measures are typical. Financial measures such as profit, ROI (return on investment), or EVA (economic value added) are also used. American Compensation Association survey results indicate that organizations report greater success with measures that take into account both operational and financial measures.[16] The employees' portion of the gain is placed in a bonus pool and is distributed either on a percentage basis of salary or on "hours worked." (The Fair Labor Standards Act regulates how nonexempt employee bonuses are computed and should be consulted before designing a bonus formula.) Almost always the bonus is paid monthly or quarterly. Often, a portion of the employees' share is put in a reserve account and used to cover any future deficits. At the end of the year, any remaining reserves are then returned to the employees. The most typical way the bonus is paid is through a separate check. These methods have withstood the test of time because they are considered fair and reasonable and are usually not difficult to design and compute.

Increasingly, some organizations take a quite different approach. They look *forward* and ask the question, "What performance is needed to achieve our objectives in the upcoming period?" They believe what was adequate in the past may no longer be adequate for the future. They do not wish to reward for improvements if the results still do not meet the continuous improvement goals they have committed to. This system is called "goal sharing" and is the approach favored by Sears and Spring Engineering. Both organizations participatively set the goals with their employees so that the employees know the goals are achievable and realistic.

Both the gainsharing and goalsharing approaches can be used by not-for-profit organizations, although unfortunately there are few examples. One of the most well known is Beth Israel Hospital–Boston, which has had a successful Scanlon system called "Prepare 21" since 1989. Beth Israel has credited its Scanlon process with helping save hundreds of thousands of dollars in cost while improving quality and patient care. One of the highlights of Beth Israel's year is the Prepare 21 Recognition program. During this time, employees and teams are recognized for their contribution to Prepare 21 and to Beth Israel. It is usually standing-room only as the busy staff of this major teaching hospital comes together to honor its own. Recipients not only receive the accolades of their peers but also have their names added permanently to a special kiosk near the hospital's cafeteria.

Other organizations feel that the only true measure of performance is profit, and so they develop profit sharing plans. Purists would argue that profit sharing is a concept foreign to a discussion of gainsharing, but philosophically the ideas are similar. Profit sharing can be considered a financial measure bonus system. Profits above a base number are split with employees. Scanlon studied profit sharing in the 1940s and concluded: "The analysis of these plans indicates that a sense of participation and partnership is the fundamental prerequisite. If this is fully developed the type of plan itself is of secondary importance."[17]

Douglas Kruse found that the adoption of profit sharing results in productivity gains of 3.5% to 5%.[18] There are two common challenges associated with profit sharing. The first is a literacy issue. Most employees simply do not understand profit and must be educated to understand what it is. The second issue is "line of sight." Profit is influenced by many factors beyond the control of the typical employee.

These challenges are not impossible, and there are many successful profit sharing programs. Wescast Industries, a Canadian company that produces most of the engine manifolds in North America, combines a once-a-year profit sharing bonus with a quarterly operational measure bonus system. This system helps to focus employees on the profitability of the corporation and at the same time on the need for quality, safety, and productivity.

Employee ownership can be combined with gainsharing, goalsharing, and profit sharing. Herman Miller has had a Scanlon system since 1950, and also provides stock to every employee with over one year of service. Max De Pree, a former CEO of Herman Miller, said, "Employee stock ownership is clearly a competitive reality. Nothing is being given. Ownership is earned and paid for. The heart of it is profit sharing, and there is no sharing if there are no profits. Risk and reward are connected logically and fairly. There is no smug condescension at play here. Rather, there is a certain morality in connecting shared accountability as employees with shared ownership. This lends a rightness and permanence to the relationship of each of us to our work and to each other."[19]

Finally, it is not necessary and maybe even counterproductive to give money as the gain. Once a bonus check is cashed and the money spent, it is often difficult for employees to know where the money went. Cerdec Corporation/Drakenfeld Products provides its employees with "mall dollars" that they can spend at local businesses. Employees can purchase goods and services from vacations to cars. A new VCR may have more "trophy value" than the equivalent in money. Employees remember what items they received in mall dollars. Enterprising organizations could even use the mall dollar concept to negotiate favorable exchanges and discounts from merchants. Most merchants would gladly offer a discount for a captive customer. An additional benefit of the concept is that money remains in the local economy.

Another creative approach is taken by Weyburn-Bartel Incorporated, which pays its bonus in meat. Employees sign up for various cuts of beef or seafood that are delivered by refrigerated truck. The system prevents the value of their bonus from being eroded by sales taxes. While this approach is not for everyone, it does show that there are many creative ways to create an equity system.

When evaluating your options, consider the following questions:

Do you wish to create a bonus system or an equity system?

- If bonus, consider Improshare®.

- If equity, consider Scanlon. Create a balanced scorecard measuring system. Make sure the bonus formula takes into account the real needs of the stakeholders. Think creatively.

Do you wish to implement gainsharing, goalsharing, or profit sharing?

- If gainsharing, you will need good historical data from which to create a baseline. Select a baseline period that takes into account your business cycle and typical performance.

- If goalsharing, you will need to participatively develop goals with employees if you want them to be realistic and accepted.

- If profit sharing, you will need to determine what measure of profit you will use. You will have to determine what level of profit will result in sharing.

Commitment to Competency

Business literacy, participation, and Theory Y management require increased employee competency. Employees must learn to do more than what is expected in traditional firms. Motorola's Scanlon philosophy has led it to invest over 50 million dollars per year (as of 1990) in employee training and development. Sears has created Sears University. When implemented as a compensation strategy, gainsharing does not identify this type of commitment to increased competency as one of its goals.

Participatory gainsharing requires changes in both managers and employees. Managers must learn how to lead, to listen, and to coach. Employees must learn how to work in teams, control quality, and reduce costs. Both employees and organizations must commit to major investments in time, energy, and money to be successful. Scanlon organizations believe the investment is worth the cost. They believe employees are an asset to be developed, not a cost to be reduced. For example, in three separate audits Motorola calculated a $30 return for every dollar invested in training and development.

At the very least, every gainsharing system must help employees to become competent in understanding the basis of the gainsharing formula that is used. If employees do not understand the calculation, they will not know why they are or are not receiving the bonus. They will view the bonus as a lottery that they hope to win but over which they have little influence.

When evaluating your options, consider the following questions:

Do you believe employees are an asset to be developed or a cost to be reduced?

- If an asset to be developed, recognize your strategy is for the long term. Consider a Scanlon process.

- If a cost to be reduced, do not consider gainsharing. Consider reengineering, automation, contracting out, or another approach as a strategy.

Mechanics of Gainsharing

Once an organization is clear on the ABCs of gainsharing, the mechanics of gainsharing become more straightforward. Every organization considering a gainsharing system should address the following mechanics before implementing it.

I. What is our reason for considering a gainsharing system; i.e., what do we seek to accomplish?
II. Do we have top management and organization commitment and support?
III. Is this the right time?
    A. Do we have enough time to design the system?
    B. Are there other issues we need to address first?
        1. Management competency
        2. Union relations
        3. Compensation system
IV. Who will create the system?
    A. Will we work with a consultant?
    B. Will we design it ourselves?
        1. How will we select the design committee(s) and what will their roles be?
        2. How will we involve the organization/union?
V. What are we trying to improve?
    A. How will we measure it?
    B. Will we have all stakeholders identified?
VI. Improvement over what?
    A. Gainsharing
        1. How will we construct the base period?
        2. What is the protection for the company?
            a. Split
            b. Reserve
            c. Caps
    B. Goalsharing
        1. How much money can we spend?
        2. What are the goals we must accomplish?
        3. How will we pay out?
    C. Profit sharing
        1. What measure of profitability will we use?
        2. How will we protect the company?
            a. Minimum profitability before sharing
            b. Split
            c. Reserves
            d. Caps
VII. Who will be covered by gainsharing?
    A. Will we include everybody?
    B. How will we take into consideration line-of-sight?
VIII. How will we communicate gainsharing to our employees?

IX. Who will maintain the system?
   A.   Do we need a gainsharing coordinator position?
   B.   How will we keep it from becoming another Human Relations department program?
 X. How will we know if gainsharing is successful?
XI. How will we change the system?

Conclusion

Gainsharing is a proven, powerful tool to manage an organization if there is an understanding of the basic ABCs of gainsharing. Mistakes are made by those that do not take the time to understand the differences between the various approaches that are available. Before beginning a gainsharing program, carefully evaluate your Assumptions about motivation. Consider the effect of Business literacy. Finally, consider the level of Commitment your organization will expect and is willing to provide. Once the basic ABCs are mastered, the right gainsharing approach for you will be much clearer.

Notes

1.   Robert Levering and Milton Moskowitz, *The 100 Best Companies to Work For in America* (New York: Doubleday, 1993).

2.   Jerry L. McAdams and Elizabeth J. Hawk, *Organizational Performance and Rewards: 663 Experiences in Making the Link* (St. Louis, Mo.: American Compensation Association and Maritz, Inc., 1994).

3.   M. Schuster, "Forty Years of Scanlon Plan Research: A Review of the Descriptive and Empirical Literature," *International Yearbook of Organizational Democracy* 1 (1983): 53-71.

4.   Dong-One Kim, "Factors Influencing Organizational Performance in Gainsharing Programs" (unpublished paper, University of Wisconsin-Madison, 1994).

5.   Alfie Kohn, *Punished by Rewards: The Trouble with Gold Stars, Incentive Plans, A's, Praise, and Other Bribes* (New York: Houghton Mifflin Company, 1993), 190.

6.   Lewis Eigen and Jonathan P. Siegel, *The Manager's Book of Quotations* (New York: AMACOM, 1989), 271.

7.   Frederick Winslow Taylor, *The Principles of Scientific Management* (1911).

8. Hugh De Pree, *Business as Unusual: The People and Principles of Herman Miller* (Zeeland: Herman Miller, 1986), 4.

9. Mitchell Fein, *Improshare: An Alternative to Traditional Managing* (American Institute of Industrial Engineers, 1981), 27.

10. Ibid., 23.

11. Jerry L. McAdams, *The Reward Plan Advantage* (San Francisco: Jossey-Bass, 1996).

12. R. Davenport, "The Greatest Opportunity on Earth," *Fortune,* October 1949; idem, "Enterprise for Everyman," *Fortune,* vol. 41, no. 1 (January 1950), 51-58.

13. Joseph Scanlon, personal correspondence, Penn State University, Steelworkers Archives.

14. Kim, "Factors Influencing Organizational Performance in Gainsharing Programs."

15. Carl Frost, "Leadership in the New American Workplace," unpublished workbook. (Scanlon Plan Associates, 1993).

16. McAdams and Hawk, *Organizational Performance and Rewards.*

17. Joseph Scanlon, "Profit Sharing under Collective Bargaining: Three Case Studies," in *The Scanlon Plan: A Frontier in Labor-Management Cooperation,* ed. Frederick G. Lesieur (Cambridge, MA: Technology Press of MIT, 1958).

18. Douglas Kruse, *Profit Sharing: Does It Make a Difference?* (Kalamazoo, Mich.: W.E. Upjohn Institute for Employment Research, 1993), vi.

19. Max De Pree, *Leadership Is an Art* (New York: Doubleday, 1987), 85. (Max De Pree is not to be confused with his brother Hugh [cited above], who preceded him as Herman Miller CEO.)

Part Two

Case Studies

Chapter 10

Incentive Programs in a Professional Services Firm

Darryl Orr

In 1993, Smith & Company was barely breaking even. It was a solid firm with a reputation for doing superior work. It paid competitive wages and offered many benefits. The firm was by no means a failure, but it was not generating significant profits. After 30 years, Samuel H. Smith, the principal owner, was growing weary of carrying most of the load.

Things began to turn around in 1994. With the establishment of an employee stock ownership plan (ESOP) and adoption of open-book management, profits have soared. The value of the business has more than doubled. Employment has increased from 24 to 35. Total employment is predicted to reach 50 people within the next three years. A new office addition has been completed. A five-year ESOP loan was paid off in two years and more stock has been purchased from Smith. The employee owners are learning about business—*their* business—and it shows. The company's finances have dramatically improved. Smith is making more money (as are the employees). More importantly, he's having more fun.

The Firm

Smith & Company, located in southeast Missouri, is a medium-size professional firm that provides civil engineering, surveying, and testing services to public and private clients. The firm, founded in 1965, employs 35 people. Smith & Company engineers design bridges, highways, airports, water systems, wastewater systems, and drainage facilities. Its surveyors perform site surveys for architects and other engineering firms, construction contractors, government agencies, and individual property owners. The testing department provides quality control on projects designed by other architectural and engineering firms as well as on Smith & Company projects. Employees' educational credentials range from high school diplomas to master's degrees in business administration or engineering. Some employees are salaried; others are hourly workers.

The Smith & Company ESOP

In 1993 the firm's principal owner, Sam Smith, decided to begin selling his stock. For several reasons, he picked an employee stock ownership plan (ESOP) to accomplish this goal. First, he could sell his stock with maximum financial and tax advantages. Second, rather than divest himself of all stock immediately, he could sell portions of stock to coincide with his plans for retirement (which was still several years in the future). Third, he could sell his stock to his own employees. After all, they, or employees like them, had helped him stay in business for 30 years.

In 1994, Smith established the ESOP and used it to borrow enough money to buy 30% of the company with a five-year note. The ESOP is conventionally structured, with stock allocation based on salary and with graduated vesting starting at 20% after three years of employment and increasing to 100% after seven years.

The basic premise behind an ESOP is that if each employee owns a part of the firm, then each employee will be motivated to make that firm thrive. When people put their money into other companies, it is an *investment*. When they own a piece of the firm where they work, it is a *commitment*.

For an ESOP to be truly successful, it is not enough to call each employee an "owner"; each employee must think of himself or herself as an owner. Commitment to the spirit of the ESOP must come from the top. Employees will think of themselves as owners only when "the Boss" thinks of them as owners. In many firms, the question is not whether or not the employees are ready for an ESOP; the question is whether or not "the Boss" is ready for an ESOP. The three main ingredients needed to instill that thinking in both parties are education, communication, and dedication.

Senior management must be dedicated to educating all employee owners by communicating all of the information needed to successfully run *their* business. To that end, Smith implemented several incentive programs, both monetary and nonmonetary, to motivate his people to increase the firm's success and to begin the educational process of changing attitudes from those of being "hired hands" to those of being "owners."

Open-Book Management and Education Programs

Open-book management is defined in Dr. Arthur R. Pell's book, *The Complete Idiot's Guide to Managing People*, as "a management style in which employees are considered full partners in the operation of a business. One characteristic of this management style is that employees have a direct stake in their company's success (if the business is profitable, they share in the profits; if not, there are no profits to share). Another characteristic is that every employee has access to numbers that are critical to tracking the company's performance and are given the training and tools to understand them."

It sounds relatively simple, doesn't it? Well, it isn't!

No conscientious parent would hand a child a set of car keys without instruction and practice on the technique of driving, at least not if the parent wanted the child *and the car* to return home safely. Likewise, managers cannot hand the "keys" of the company over to employees unskilled in business. Education must come first. As employees become more and more proficient in ownership, more and more responsibility can and should be turned over to them.

Any worthwhile endeavor, especially education, requires real effort, persistence, skill, and leadership. Management cannot just throw a monthly financial statement out on the table in front of the employees and say, "Here's the open book, think like owners." Opening the books is the easy part; teaching everyone to understand those books and the business is much more difficult.

Installing the ESOP at Smith & Company went smoothly. The next step, making ownership part of our corporate thinking, was more difficult, even painful to some. Change scares many people. According to Kenneth Blanchard, author of *The One Minute Manager* and several other books, when people are asked to do something different, they focus on what they have to give up, not on what they are going to gain. People have several concerns when asked to change. Their first concern is for *information:* What do you have in mind? Am I free to ask questions? The second concern is *personal:* What is going to happen to me? Will I survive this change? The third concern is *implementation:* How is the change going to be done? The fourth concern is *impact:* What will this change cost financially and emotionally? What is the benefit?

Some employees, including one senior manager, left the firm. Some had grown comfortable with the "old way of doing things." Some said that they wanted to concentrate on their job, not the business; they could not understand or accept that the two were inseparable. The daily scorecard distributed to everyone in the company showed who was hitting their billable target and who was not. Some did not like having their productivity, or lack of it, measured.

Little is written about the people who do not want the responsibility of ownership; however, every firm has some of those people. Some people develop an ownership mentality slower than others; some never do. Many times, they are excellent workers and are an asset to the firm in every other way. They cannot and should not be written off or dismissed. They have their place in an open-book management firm, although they will miss out on a lot of fun. Sadly, some good people move on to other firms and a different vision. On the positive side, some not-so-good people leave as well.

Weekly Management and Department Meetings

To begin the educational process, Smith started meeting weekly with managers to discuss business and ESOP issues. These managers then met weekly with their departments to relay the information to all employees. These meetings continue and are vital to getting the word out and keeping everyone involved in the day-to-day business at Smith & Company.

Monthly Company Meetings

Each month a company-wide meeting is held to discuss business. Topics may include finances, marketing, new projects, possible projects, five-year growth projections, department head reports, committee reports, and anything else people want to cover. Although participation is voluntary, attendance is generally 100%.

Monthly Financial Meetings

Just a day or two before each monthly company meeting, when the financial statements are received from our outside accounting firm, voluntary Tuesday and Wednesday evening meetings are conducted to review finances. About 60 to 75% of the employees attend these financial meetings.

At first, Smith conducted these financial meetings himself. In his words, that approach had "zero credibility," which hurt; some of those skeptical employees had worked with him for a long time. He knew he was being honest and was giving the employees a true picture of the company's finances. But rather than dwell on the skepticism, he moved ahead by assigning five people at random to study the financial statements. They met with the firm's outside CPA and then picked one person to make the presentation at the next company meeting. The financials got credibility. Now different volunteers make the presentations at each of the two monthly financial meetings.

In addition to increased credibility, letting various people give the financial presentations helps more people learn the financials well enough to explain them to others. Before you can teach a subject well, you first have to learn it. More of our people are made a part of the process; their business education is advanced.

Advantages: People learn about business; specifically, they learn about *their* business. People learn that what they do affects the "bottom line"; they become financially responsible.

Disadvantages: Numbers are boring, boring, boring to some people. CPAs have their own language, a language that many people find utterly foreign and confusing, with terms such as "assets and liabilities," "stock equity," "accounts receivable," and "accumulated depreciation." People tend not to trust things they do not understand. It takes effort, skill, and time to make financial presentations interesting and credible. It also takes a lot of patience.

The Balanced Daily Scorecard

According to a recent review in the August 19, 1996, issue of *Open-Book Management Bulletin,* published by Open-Book Management, Inc., authors Robert S. Kaplan and David P. Norton assert in their new book, *The Balanced Scorecard* (Boston: Harvard Business School Press, 1996), that companies need a variety of measures to monitor their success. A company must focus on numbers that "translate a business unit's mission and strategy into tangible objectives and measures." Financial objectives must be linked to strategic goals, such as expanding your customer base by 20%. A *balanced scorecard* is essential in ensuring that financial goals have a business rationale.

According to Kaplan and Norton, financial targets must be linked to what they call "performance drivers." External performance drivers include such measures as customer satisfaction, customer retention, new-customer acquisition, and customer profitability. Internal performance drivers focus on business processes and measure quality, delivery time, and labor productivity. Drivers can be long-term or short-term. Simply put, external drivers concentrate on the customer; internal drivers concentrate on the employee. A successful company must concentrate on both. To keep the customer happy you must keep the employee happy. Focusing exclusively on financial returns leads to oblivion.

Certain key numbers—in the case of professional services firms, *billable hours*—will move the bottom line in the right direction. Employees need to understand the link between profit/loss and billable hours. Everyone, managers and employees, must understand that it is not enough to have high billable rates; the work must also be completed within budget and on time. In other words, employees must not just bill time to a project; they must complete the project. Managers and employees must track each project assigned to them to assure that it gets "out the door" on time and within the fee.

To reach our profit goals, we must bill the hours; however, to keep the customer happy (and earn future profits), we must satisfy the customer's needs by delivering a good quality product on time and within budget.

Incentive Programs and the Great Game of Business

The Great Game of Business

To survive, a business must do two things: (1) make money and (2) generate cash. Everything else is a means to that end. Smith was introduced to this simple concept in 1993 at a "Great Game of Business" ("Great Game") seminar conducted by representatives of Springfield ReManufacturing Corporation (SRC) in Springfield, Missouri. He had been steered in SRC's direction when attending an ESOP seminar earlier that year in Memphis, Tennessee.

After returning from that Great Game seminar, Smith began to plant the seeds of the Great Game at Smith & Company. Smith bought copies of Jack Stack's book *The Great Game of Business* and distributed them to his managers. After reading it, Smith and his managers discussed how to introduce the Great Game to the other employees. In the beginning the games were modest.

Smith & Company, like most professional service firms, makes its money selling its billable hours. Time sheets were turned in daily, although some people would fall two or three days behind. In 1993, billable hours were not as high as we felt they could be;

the firm was barely breaking even. We needed a game that would increase our billable hours. Obviously, this would increase our income and consequently our profit. Our first game was set up before our ESOP, but we really started getting into the games after the ESOP. The games help us *understand* the business; the ESOP helps us *think* like business owners.

Setting up the game was crucial; it would mean the difference between the game being the *management's* game or the *employees'* game. Anything perceived to be the management's game would probably be doomed to failure. Thus, every employee was involved in the process. Every employee was asked: How many billable hours per week did he or she think were reasonable for him or her to achieve? After input from each employee, the billable hours "target" of each employee was then multiplied by that employee's hourly billable rate. Then, based on everyone's individual target, the billable income of every employee was totaled to determine the firm's monthly billable income. We had our first goal; hit that total monthly billable income and everybody would get a bonus.

That first month—December 1993—we played for a bonus of $100 per person. Each day the billable hours and billable income for each employee were tabulated on a chart—our *scorecard.* The scorecard was passed out to every employee every day. Everyone knew where they, and the company, stood. The increase in billable hours was immediate, even beyond what people said they could do. We made our first goal; we got our $100. We had stopped the decline; profit was headed up. Some people started thinking that there just might be something to this Great Game of Business.

The Bigger Bucket of Bucks Game

We do not ignore monetary rewards. In fact, we love to give away money to ourselves—as long as it comes from our profits. We've played for "Bucks" and "Buckets of Bucks." We are now playing for "Bigger Buckets of Bucks." In 1994 we hit our annual goal by the end of the third quarter and distributed $50,000 in bonuses. In 1995, $77,500 was handed out. Five buckets had been budgeted in 1996; however, adding a second floor and eight offices to our building and installing a computer network decreased productivity. Even so, three profit goals (buckets) were met in 1996 and $42,500 was distributed in bonuses. The new building addition and the computer network have helped us to increase productivity substantially this year; we are back on track.

Our main monetary game—Bigger Bucket of Bucks—is based on profit goals (six buckets) that are set at the beginning of the year. When we reach a preset profit (fill a bucket), as determined by monthly financial reports prepared by our accounting firm, a portion of that profit is distributed to each employee based on salary. We make that a big deal. The bonus is handed out to each employee at our monthly company meeting, and then we celebrate our success with a cookout. Sometimes caps or jackets or T-shirts with the company logo are handed out to everyone to underscore the achievement. Company photographs are taken; sometimes the press is invited. We want people, including our clients, to know that we are a successful employee-owned company. Up to now, profit goals have been set by senior management. However, during the preparation of the annual budget, each department head and each of the company's six committees are asked to contribute their estimates of the next year's expenses and income. As the employee-owners' business knowledge increases, so does their involvement in budget preparation and game development.

Advantages: Monetary games keep our people interested in the "bottom line." Open-book management and the ESOP are based on everyone's sharing in the success or failure of the company. When the firm is profitable, bonuses keep that promise.

Disadvantages: It can be argued that money alone can be more of a de-motivator than a motivator. There is more to the success of a company than profits. Concentrating only on the bottom line can lead to substandard work, unhappy customers, and disgruntled employees. An unhappy company is not a successful company no matter how much money it makes. Of course, it should also be pointed out that a company that is losing money is more likely to have disgruntled employees producing substandard work that leads to unhappy customers.

The Accounts Receivable Game

Games are used to target and solve specific problems. For example, our company had an accounts receivable (A/R) problem. We were making money (profits were up), but we weren't generating cash. Our A/R (money owed us) exceeded 20% of our total annual billings. On paper, we were doing great. We were making money, but every now and then Smith still had to call our banker to borrow money to make the payroll. We had to pay interest on that borrowed money, interest that came out of our profits.

Everyone connected to billing—engineers, managers, department heads, and bookkeeper—was gathered together. Smith explained the problem very simply: the firm needed cash. The group was divided into five teams; each team was given a list of past-due accounts that were outstanding for at least 30 days. Special emphasis was placed on collecting those overdue accounts. The mission was to reduce the accounts receivable to 15% of our total annual billings and keep it there for three months. If they were successful, each team member would get $100 cash.

Some collections were as simple as making a phone call; some took a letter or the resubmittal of the invoice. Some required meeting with the client to resolve a misunderstanding. Slowly but surely, the A/R is decreasing; we are generating cash. We will pay out $1,700 in bonuses but save $6,000 in interest. Another lesson in business will be learned.

Advantages: It teaches our people that it is just as important to generate cash as it is to make money. It makes everyone, not just Smith and the bookkeeper, responsible for and interested in collecting the money due us.

Disadvantages: Many people hate to collect money; they feel that it burdens them with a very unpleasant task. It can take engineers and managers away from "billable" work, which decreases productivity. A "Catch 22" is that the more successful a firm is at billing its time, the more A/R it generates and a certain portion of that increased A/R will become overdue. It seems to be easier to make money than to generate cash; however, it is easier to generate cash when you are making money than when you are losing it.

Nonmonetary Incentive Programs

The monetary incentive programs are not so much designed to inspire our people as they are to keep people interested in the business. In fact, money alone is not usually a very good motivator in the long run. The key to inspiring people is not throwing money at them; it is throwing appreciation at them. Another key is providing a structure, an opportunity, that allows people to do a very good job. People are *interested* in making money but people are *inspired* by such things as opportunity and knowing that they are successful and being recognized for a job well done. The best incentive programs provide those things.

At Smith & Company, we look for reasons to celebrate. Engineering is a serious business; lots of money, even lives, can hang in the balance. Our people work hard. The work demands concentration and attention to detail; therefore, to prevent burnout, our people need to unwind from time to time. We invent "Little Games" toward that end. For example, we may set a *daily billable income* target; when we hit it, the department heads cook breakfast for everyone. Get people together; have fun! Remember, it's called the Great *Game* of Business.

Our games are also designed to encourage teamwork by concentrating on company-wide goals. Everyone must be involved in the business to make it a success. The company is only as strong as its weakest link; every job, every function, every employee is critical to that strength. Everyone has to realize that we sink or swim together.

Most people want to be challenged. Incentive programs should be designed to encourage high performance. Successful companies are not made up of average employees. Time after time, our people have set goals for themselves that even management thought were unattainable. Time after time, management has been proven wrong. An $8,000 billable day was set as a goal; we hit it! Then an $8,500 day; we hit it! A $9,000 day; a $10,000 day; a $40,000 week; a $45,000 week; we hit them all. It seems that the sky is the limit. Sometimes, the best thing a manager can do is just get out of the way and let a person do his or her job.

Keep the games simple. Do not try to solve all of your company's problems with one game. Keep in mind that the size of the prize is not important; it is showing appreciation for a job well done that motivates people. A good memory lasts longer than cash.

Advantages: People are kept interested in the business. Problems are solved. The games can be challenging and still be fun. They can be used to improve morale and foster teamwork.

Disadvantages: It takes time and effort to administrate the games. New games are demanded after the completion of the old ones. Employee owners will challenge you to challenge them. Sometimes having fun is hard work.

Work Teams

Each employee serves on one or more work teams of his or her choice. Team members gather at luncheon meetings—most of the time the lunch is paid for by the firm—to discuss their team's function, such as long-range planning, outside activities, the building and grounds, computers and office equipment, and vehicles and field equipment. We have a team looking into areas for the firm to expand or diversify into (some of the golfers want to open a golf pro shop). The work teams make their recommendations to the management staff at one of the weekly meetings. They are expected to present costs of implementation as well as the pros and cons of their recommendation. Each recommendation is carefully considered, and if the idea seems feasible, it is introduced to all employees for further discussion at our monthly company meeting.

All work team recommendations are taken seriously. They are discussed and sound reasons are given if an idea cannot be implemented. The intent is to allow all employees to have a say in the direction that the company takes.

Advantages: More people are involved in the running of the company. Management has a larger pool from which to draw good ideas. People learn that implementing an idea or program, even an excellent one, requires money, time, and effort. They learn that due to the cost or some other valid reason, not every idea or program can be implemented. It helps them understand that in business, as in life, there are consequences that must be considered before action can be taken.

Disadvantages: Work team members may put a lot of time and effort into ideas that cannot be implemented. This can lead to disappointment and, if not handled correctly by management, to the feeling that the teams are merely window dressing and that the employees are not thought of as "real" owners. Sometimes a work team might develop a vested interest in keeping the team intact even after its mission has been completed. If so, the team is in danger of becoming a committee; committees tend to turn into bureaucracies.

Opening the Books Wider

Almost 80% of our people have computers on their desks. Because we are networked, every person is able to tap into the company's bookkeeping program; this means that almost every employee has access to the day-to-day finances of the company. With a few keystrokes, a person can find out how much money was taken in that day or how much money was spent. They know how much time has been spent on every ongoing project and how much fee remains. They have access to information that is available only to a select few in most firms. Communication is easier, which has led to increased interest in the business.

The Future

We start planning for the next year around the middle of the present year. With everyone involved, a new budget is prepared and more new games and different incentive programs are designed. We want games and programs to encourage improved performance by rewarding such improvements. They should encourage learning more about our business by focusing attention on the right numbers.

We hope to initiate individual incentive programs, peer-recognition award programs, bigger and better bonus plans, and family recognition programs—all designed by our employee owners.

Individual Incentive Programs

At Smith & Company, managers are encouraged to informally recognize and express appreciation to individuals for outstanding achievement; however, to date we have avoided emphasis on "official" individual incentive programs. It is very hard to overcome the "us against them" attitude that tends to occur in any company. For example, there may be feelings of "hourly versus salaried" or "surveyors versus engineers" or "managers versus employees."

Some of us are concerned that by rewarding individuals or departments, we will destroy the teamwork that is necessary to accomplish our company-wide goals. However, we also realize that even in a company where almost everyone is involved in the business, there are individuals who contribute more than their fair share. They work longer or harder or more efficiently than other employees. If a firm truly wants people to be better than average, then it must find a way to encourage better-than-average performance. You receive the type of performance that you reward. Treating everyone the same encourages mediocrity.

The danger of formal individual recognition programs is that one person or department might be set against another. After all, when one person "wins" an individual award, that means all other employees have "lost" that award. If cutthroat competition results, teamwork will go out the window. There is also the danger that individuals or departments will be conditioned to narrowly focus on their own success at the expense of the company. The system might become "political" or become a personality-over-substance contest. To avoid that, our first step will be to recruit a team made up of a representative cross-section of our employees to come up with an individual incentive program. Any acceptable incentive program must balance individual incentives with company-wide incentives. It must promote cooperative effort.

We feel that the employee team might be able to develop a program that is more likely to be considered fair by all employees than if the program was developed by senior management. That means faster buy-in to that program and greater chance of success without resulting in the "us against them" attitude. We intend to proceed with great caution.

Peer-Recognition Award Program

Soon, a formal award program will be implemented that will honor employees who show a positive attitude or go "above and beyond the call of duty" to help a client or someone else within the firm. The nominations will come from co-workers who witness the outstanding efforts. The company will even have an award program for the employee who comes up with a catchy name for this peer-recognition program.

Bigger and Better Bonus Programs

In the past, our bonuses have been based on salary. For example, each person got 10% of his or her salary; therefore, the higher the salary, the bigger the bonus. Some lesser-paid employees feel cheated because their bonuses are smaller. As a consequence, for some people the positive impact of the bonus is lessened; their motivation to succeed is decreased.

To rectify that problem, a new bonus plan is needed. All employees are being encouraged to submit ideas for new and improved bonus plans. One plan under consideration is to pay out 25% of the bonus pool in equal shares and 75% based on salary. Whatever the bonus plan, it must accomplish three things: (1) motivate people, (2) help them learn the business, and (3) focus attention on the right numbers.

Family Recognition Programs

It is common in a professional services firm to request that an employee work extra hours to complete an important project or to attend a client's after-hours meeting or attend an overnight conference. While that employee's sacrifice is sometimes recognized by management, the sacrifice of his or her family goes unrecognized. The missed dinners, the missed birthday parties, the missed ball games, and so on all add up. Without the support of the family, it is very difficult for an employee to continue making that extra effort.

We intend to develop a program to recognize the sacrifice made by an employee's family. It might be something as simple as writing a note to the employee's family thanking them for support, acknowledging the good work their family member has done, and explaining the importance of the project to the company. Perhaps the employee and his or her family will be given a gift certificate for dinner in a nice restaurant or maybe even an all-expense-paid weekend retreat for the family. The size or type of gift is relatively unimportant; what is important is that the sacrifice be recognized by the company.

Conclusion

An ESOP gives the company to the employees; open-book management gives them the information needed to run it; incentive and education programs teach them to be successful. One will not work without the others. Education takes communication and dedication by everyone.

The process of going from "employee" to "owner" is slow and at times even painful. The education process must never end. Installing an ESOP and adopting open-book management does not eliminate a firm's day-to-day problems. It does not eliminate the need for managing your company or its employees. But opening the books does make management easier in many respects by changing the attitude of employees. When your employees become your partners, the workload and responsibility are spread around. You are no longer solely responsible for the success of the company.

When everyone shares in the company's future, whether good or bad, it does not take long for people to see that they will reap benefits when the future is good. In fact, employee owners will work very hard to make that future good. Smith & Company's experience with an ESOP and open-book management proves it.

Recommended Reading

Scott Adams, *The Dilbert Principle* (New York: Harper Business, 1996).

Kenneth Blanchard and Spencer Johnson, *The One Minute Manager* (Berkley Books, 1981).

John Case, *Open-Book Management: The Coming Business Revolution* (New York: Harper Business, 1995).

Bob Nelson, *1001 Ways to Reward Employees* (New York: Workman Publishing, 1994).

Dr. Arthur R. Pell, *The Complete Idiot's Guide to Managing People* (Alpha Books, 1995).

John Schuster, Jill Carpenter, and Patricia Kane, *The Power of Open-Book Management* (New York: John Wiley & Sons, 1996).

Jack Stack, *The Great Game of Business* (New York: Currency Books, 1992).

Using the Scanlon Plan in an ESOP Company

Bill Nicholson and Neil N. Koenig

Employee stock ownership plan (ESOP) companies understandably encourage pride of ownership. Initially, the emphasis is on the employees' equity stake in the company: "We're employee owners!" This is usually followed by management efforts to instill job ownership: "We do our jobs as if we owned them!" The payoff for this ownership is typically in the future—a handsome retirement fund exceeding the norm of non-ESOP retirees, assuming the ESOP company is successful in the long run.

There are a couple of problems with the deferred nature of the ESOP benefit, however. The first is that between now and retirement, employees have urgent day-to-day financial needs, and companies in today's economy cannot afford high labor costs. Market competition and international competitors' low wages have made the yearly pay raise a thing of the past. So how do companies keep costs down and still reward their employees?

The other problem with the deferred nature of the ESOP benefit is that it often is of little help with the challenge of motivating employees on a day-to-day basis. For all but the small percentage who are truly self-motivated, something more is needed than the expected biweekly paycheck and a rare remark of recognition. This is especially critical now when the routine day-to-day work is more demanding and exacting than anything most employees have ever done in their lives. Pep talks, piecework, preaching, and pizzas have all been tried and found wanting. So how do we motivate the employees who require external motivators (the majority, we fear) as conditions created by the economy and competitors demand more and more of them?

What Companies Are Looking For

Companies have long looked for ways to reward and encourage worker commitment. Additionally, companies today are looking for ways to avoid reinforcing the entitlement mentality. What we all seek are ways to provide immediate, tangible rewards based on merit. Merit means the reward is earned—truly earned. Rewards should be given for results, quality linked to quantity, effort teamed with smarts, and ideas translated into customer service.

In addition, companies want to discourage internal and individual competition that siphons off energy and effort on behalf of the whole. What is key is rewarding work that contributes to the whole: "We compete with other companies, not with each other. In here we work together if we want to win."

Companies today seek a group incentive plan based on results achieved by all working together for the entire company. The reward must be tangible, in the form of real money. And the reward must be frequent; a reward delayed is a reward forgotten.

A Partnership Approach to Group Incentive Plans

The compelling, simple logic of ESOPs is the partnership among all groups within the company. ESOPs need to be run as partnerships between management and front-line workers, operations and sales, manufacturing and marketing, veterans and newcomers, men and women: "We're all partners in this. That's how we succeed." Establishing a group incentive plan is the perfect opportunity for an ESOP company to prove its partnership approach to doing business.

Incentive plans are no place to practice top-down management. To do so is to revert to traditional parent-child paternalistic condescension: "If you eat your vegetables we'll increase your allowance." As with anything, it is best to make people insiders regarding a group incentive plan. This is especially true when it comes to money, let alone money for which employees must work hard while wages and full employment are held in check.

Incentive plans work best when everyone has bought in on the plan and in effect "owns" the plan. This means that management and front-line workers must participate together in selecting an appropriate group bonus plan. This requires an educational effort concerning the economic, business, market, and financial realities facing the company, as well as education about group incentive plans. The goal, after all, is to have everyone capable of thinking, deciding, and acting as businesspersons. This educational effort is best done both in person and in writing.

The first step is to sell the idea of a group incentive plan. Groups no larger than 30 or so employees from across the company should meet with executive leaders for crisp, clear presentations about the big-picture realities and the possibilities afforded by a group incentive plan. A genuine question-and-answer period must be part of these sessions.

The second step is to establish a recommendation committee. Ideally it would be comprised of one senior leader, two middle or supervisory managers, and four front-line partners, each peer group selecting its own representatives. Any appearance that the group incentive plan idea itself or the best plan for the company is a management gimmick or fad or ploy of the company to get more out of its employees for nothing will doom the effort. Here is where the ESOP partnership referred above serves as a role model. The committee is authorized to study, select, and present the best and most appropriate options to the company.

The third step is to reconvene the larger groups as in step one. Members of the recommendation committee present the options, including their opinion of what the most favorable option is. Each option's pros and cons are outlined. Each option is examined for how it would work and what it would mean in real money earned.

Emphasis is also needed on what now would be required of everyone—from ideas for increased productivity, cost cutting, and increased efficiencies to greater cooperation and multidisciplined approaches to solving and preventing problems. Time for genuine questions and answers is critical, as are handouts that clearly and easily spell out the contents of the presentation of the recommendation committee.

The fourth and final step is selection across the company. This can be done by individual voting or by group consensus in small meetings conducted by members of the recommendation committee.

The entire process, from step one through step four, should take no longer than a month. Any longer and momentum is lost. Any less and skepticism is engendered: "They're trying to push something down our throats again."

It is best to treat the adoption of a group incentive plan as a year-long experiment. The speed of change in today's business world requires continual evaluation and improvement anyway. And twelve monthly results should even out seasonal variables. A one-year commitment also shows confidence and courage: "As partners we can make a difference in the year ahead. And we'll reward ourselves as we go along. We can do it!"

The Distribution Company and Its $9.75 Experiment

An American distributor of building materials (the company wishes to remain anonymous) has benefited from a group incentive plan since 1975. It has 200 employees, is 100% ESOP owned, is an industry leader, and is strong financially in the cycle-sensitive world of residential and commercial construction. The company considers its management style to be participative and encourages employee involvement in the business. This is done in both structured and unstructured meetings, regular work group meetings, ad-hoc problem-solving meetings, and frequent lunch meetings with executive leaders. Leaders have dubbed the latter give-and-take meetings as "LBEL"—Leadership By Eating Lunch.

The management of the company made a conscious decision to be more participative in the early 1970s in response to an unsuccessful effort by front-line workers to unionize. A planning session that included all plant employees resulted. The number-one issue identified at this pivotal meeting was the desire for an incentive plan.

A committee of employees was drawn from both the shop floor and the administrative offices. It considered the possibilities for an incentive plan, coming up with three alternatives. The first was piecework, which is hard to measure in the distribution business and has the tendency to overemphasize individual competition. The second alternative was profit sharing; the committee's objection here was the difficulty of controlling the payoff.

The best fit for the company, the committee concluded, was a group incentive plan. They discovered the Scanlon Plan, dating from the early 1930s, in Douglas MacGregor's classic, *The Human Side of Enterprise*, published in 1960. Research in the local library turned up an article on the Parker Pen Company's use of the Scanlon Plan. Parker Pen was contacted. It identified its consultant as Fred Lesieur, who happened to have been an associate of the late Joseph Scanlon. Lesieur felt there was no need to get together: "Just read my book" (Fred G. Lesieur, *The Scanlon Plan: A Frontier in Labor-Management Cooperation* [Cambridge: MIT Press, 1958]). He sent his book for $8.00. The phone call cost $1.75. From this $9.75 investment the distributor worked out its own simplified version of the Scanlon Plan, implementing it on January 1, 1975. The company was proud to proceed without expensive outside consultants, going forward with employee participants practicing partnership—this in the wake of the recent union threat.

The Adapted Scanlon Plan

The distributor discovered as it studied the Scanlon Plan that it is more than an incentive formula. It should be looked at as a system of management because it involves a formal feedback system. Rather than adopting the Plan indiscriminately, it added the Plan's feedback system to its own management system, continuing to emphasize especially the participative, partnership approach to running the company.

The company's plan rewards productivity as a function of the interplay between labor costs (payroll) and current sales. Current sales were chosen because turnaround time in distributing is so rapid. Thus, the formula in use has been payroll divided by current sales.

The company investigated its performance over the years and calculated its historical standard for payroll as a percentage of sales (12% in the example below). The percentage is set by the employees themselves and is reviewed annually. Hence, incentive payments come from new profits.

The bonus is measured and paid monthly to provide immediate and continuous feedback. The bonus is paid in cash, in checks separate from regular payroll checks. Fifty percent is paid monthly and the other half is retained to cover months when seasonal fluctuations occur. Anything left over at the end of the year is paid as a year-end bonus. Payroll is not leveled for vacations and holidays. New workers must wait 18 months to qualify for participation in the plan. There are monthly and annual reports, in keeping with the financial educational needs of partnership-style management.

To illustrate, let us suppose that annual sales are $1 million and that 12% is the historical standard for payroll as a percentage of sales. That gives an allowed payroll of $120,000 (12% of $1 million). Actual payroll turns out to be $100,000, leaving a $20,000 pool of bonus money to be divided among the employees. The company retains 25% (here, $5,000) and the employees get 75% (here, $15,000). Of this amount to be divided among the employees, half is paid out immediately (here, $7,500) and the other half is placed in a reserve account for the rainy-day months and, if anything is left, the year-end bonus (table 11-1).

Variations of Group Incentive Plans

The Scanlon Plan rewards productivity as measured by payroll as a percentage of sales. As the Scanlon Plan has evolved, some companies have modified the original ratio to include additional costs

Table 11-1. How the Scanlon Plan Works at the Distribution Company

Sales	$1,000,000
Historical standard for payroll as % of sales (12%)	× .12
Allowed payroll	120,000
Actual payroll	(100,000)
Bonus pool	20,000
Employee share (75% of bonus pool)	15,000
Reserve account (50%)	(7,500)
Monthly bonus to be paid	$ 7,500

so that participants do not focus on one cost at the expense of another. For example, a person on a grinding machine found that he could improve the payroll-to-sales ratio by tightening the wheel and increasing the speed in the process. While the payroll-to-sales ratio improved, the cost of replacing the grinding wheels increased and total company performance declined. Other companies have included the cost of payroll and damage as a percentage of sales. Sales can be net of customer returns, which includes a customer service focus in the ratio. Some manufacturers have found a ratio of payroll to the sales value of production to be better, as their productivity is related to production, not shipment.

As companies tailor-make their group incentive plans, they must not overlook other costs for short-term gain at the expense of long-term strategies. This requires an environment of ongoing dialogue about the business (e.g., the lunch meetings discussed above) so that people understand how to build the business for long-term success.

A principle of the Scanlon Plan is that the standard of performance is current results. The standard, therefore, has been set by the participants, not an outside resource. Our distributor decided that the best representation of current performance was the average of the last two years. A caution is called for: Some companies have implemented the plan in an economic downturn. Consequently, current performance would be based on unusually low productivity. This would result in productivity bonuses paid before they were warranted, a detriment to the company and therefore to the participants.

Another important principle of the Scanlon Plan is that the ratio is reviewed annually and adjusted for extenuating circumstances. This is the case, for example, when productivity gains are from technology. The intent is to reward participants for gains in *their* productivity, encouraging an environment of working smarter, not harder. Our distributor once changed the ratio during a period of severe economic downturn so that productivity bonuses were not paid while the company was below a break-even point.

Making the Group Incentive Plan Work

At the company we have discussed, the plan is explained to employees as follows: "The plan adjusts the company's pay structure to its ability to pay—if we've got it, we'll pay it; if we don't, we can't and won't." Under the plan, payroll becomes a variable cost. The issue for employees is to choose between fewer people earning more money or more people earning less money. The cost to the company is the same.

Because the plan makes the money paid to workers a variable, sales-driven cost, it allows the company to avoid major work-force cuts when revenues are down. This prevents the company from losing experienced, trained employees, and is a very important advantage both for the company and for the employees who would otherwise be laid off during major downturns. A further advantage is the merit-based reward that is at the heart of this incentive plan. The harder people work, the smarter they work, the more creatively they work, and the more efficiently they work, the more the reward is. Entitlement, politics, and seniority have nothing to do with the reward. The employees themselves must make the incentive pay.

The President/CEO of the distributorship in this discussion related how business early in the year was slow, employees becoming "crabby," as he put it—their way of expressing boredom, frustration with not being challenged, and some fear that perhaps the summer would not be busy. "And people were grousing that incentive pay wasn't as it was in the good old days," he added. When business dramatically picked up in July, the President/CEO sent out the following message to every employee:

> Want to earn a 25% bonus this month? It can be done. Let's not lose sight of the fact that WE have to MAKE the incentive pay. Here's how August can be a 25% bonus: Our average invoicing for the last 9 days is $225,000 per day. If we can ship 10% more a day in August, with the same crew and the same hours, the incentive earnings will be 25%—half paid in September and half paid with the year-end bonus.
>
> If we can do that and reduce errors, we don't have to waste money correcting them—and the incentive rises.
>
> How many people do you know that have the opportunity to earn an additional 25% this month? I think the answer is not many. This is the place where that opportunity exists—and if we don't take advantage of it, we will have missed a big chance.

The President/CEO says, "Everyone in the company had this in their hands on August 1. Based on the feedback I've gotten, including feedback at several of our LBEL meetings, this really created some excitement."

By mid-October the President/CEO summarized how their modified Scanlon Plan worked out as a group incentive plan: "We have been at absolute peak for about eight weeks, and we are doing just fine. We have gone from twice a week lunch meetings to twice a month—we wanted to keep track of the company's temperature, but didn't really have time for too many meetings. The refrain still comes up: 'We're at our best when we are busy.' The main problem areas this summer were where we were working too many hours. We were really staffed lean. But it was the employees' decision. So when the September incentive checks came out, the hours didn't seem to be so long after all. We had a lot of tired but happy workers around here. Proud, too. And remember, we had absolutely no help from price increases. In fact, our prices are 1% lower than last year. And we incurred some cost increases as well. Yet we made our merit increases. In spite of how tough the environment is to operate in, our people did great. They deserved their bonus."

Chapter 12

A Two-Tier Equity Incentive Program at Apex Systems

Bryan Girard

While the concept of temporary staffing is not new, Apex Systems of Richmond, VA, is unusual in that all its employees enjoy a degree of ownership rarely seen in that industry. The company was founded in 1995 by Brian Callaghan, Win Sheridan, and Jeff Veatch, all of whom had spent many years with companies that failed to provide their employees with the opportunity to think and act like owners. The trio set about instituting programs designed to enrich the lives, careers, and compensation of the employees, knowing that this would produce happier, more productive workers.

Largely as a result of these efforts, Apex grew by 3,900% over the first five years and has continued growing steadily since, even as many of their peers went out of business or experienced significant losses. The staff has expanded from the original three founders to 428 internal employees and more than 2,200 contractors distributed throughout 20 offices serving about 500 clients. Apex achieved nearly $120 million in revenue in 2004, up from $82 million the previous year. The company is expecting another banner year for 2005, projecting a 35% growth in revenues.

Providing Suitable Rewards

It is important to understand that technical staffing is a viciously competitive business, especially during the high-tech boom times of recent years. Experienced programmers, designers, and engineers often have a broad range of highly compensated job opportunities, and many are aggressively recruited by placement firms. The challenge for Apex was to find a way to *meaningfully* augment compensation for its 400-plus permanent employees while still maintaining its status as a privately held S corporation.

The answer was a twofold solution consisting of a stock appreciation rights (SAR) program and incentive stock options (ISOs), both of which were rolled out on January 1, 1999.

SAR Program Motivates and Rewards

The SAR program is intended as a broad-based rewards plan and is designed primarily for the approximately 100 direct sales staff and 220 in-house recruiters. It is more flexible than a true option plan, avoids the limits placed on the maximum number of S corporation shareholders, and allows Apex to allocate varying amounts to the recipients. Moreover, they can borrow against their account balances and always have the ability to cash out entirely. All employees eligible for the SAR must achieve predetermined levels of performance before receiving any appreciation rights. For this reason, Apex calls its plan the "Top Performers Equity Plan." The SAR is indexed to Apex's stock appreciation by means of a formula that was devised by an outside committee comprised of industry experts, attorneys, and accountants. The formula produces a per-share value based on the company's EBIT (earnings before interest and taxes) as certified by an annual independent audit.

ISOs Encourage Growth

Just before 1999, when Apex was active in only five cities, management recognized that rapid growth would come only from geographic expansion and this would mean permanently relocating experienced managers to open up new regions. Considered something of a hardship, this assignment warranted motivation and reward beyond that provided by the SAR. An ISO plan was designed to focus on the first 36 months—the time required to launch and lead a new office into profitability. At the same time, the ISOs could serve to recruit, retain, and reward senior managers. There are currently 17 optionees, none of whom has yet exercised any options. While the plan stipulates no formal vesting period, Apex applies vesting restrictions on a case-by-case basis.

Communicating the Message

In keeping with Apex's philosophy about employee involvement, every effort is made to ensure that employees are kept up to date as to the company's performance and the value of the stock. There are quarterly "all-hands" meetings at each of the 20 branch offices, as well as major meetings at the mid-point and end of each year to set targets and performance standards and to report on the company's financial position. "Communication is an everyday job," says Apex CFO, Ted Hanson. "People are not going to feel involved if they are uninformed."

The company's generous attitude towards the staff does not end with its permanent employees. Whereas in most technical staffing companies, contractors do not receive benefits—they are expected to be independent, self-sufficient business men and women and are treated accordingly—Apex disagrees with this approach. All Apex contractors can participate in a richly matched 401(k) plan in which (and this is very unusual) the contractor is immediately 100% vested once he or she begins contributing; they are also eligible for major medical health insurance, a Section 125 "cafeteria plan," overtime pay, and referral bonuses. The end result has been a very high reengagement rate, a good indicator that the contractors like working for Apex.

In an industry that has at times earned itself a less-than-stellar reputation by shunting people in and out the door with little regard for their welfare, Apex Systems has prospered by recognizing the fundamental truth of employee ownership: people need to feel valued, involved and respected. And when they do, they will act as owners rather than expendable hourly workers. As CFO Hanson puts it, "We wanted to create real wealth for our employees; after all, in our business they're all we've got."

Chapter 13

Growing Toward a Total Rewards Portfolio at Intuit

Bryan Girard

In the field of personal and small business finance automation, there is one dominant player whose name is immediately recognizable to almost everybody. The company is Intuit Inc., and there are some very good reasons for its dramatic success.

Intuit was founded by Scott Cook and Tom Proulx in Silicon Valley back in the days when technology was still very much a gamble, and access to venture capital required a sound business plan and solid management expertise to back it up. The founders foresaw the need for inexpensive and easy-to-use software to assist in personal finance and tax planning. The advent of the personal computer enabled them to realize their vision and make it available to the ordinary householder.

Founded in 1983, Intuit now has 13 major U.S. locations and offices in seven countries. It has grown into a publicly traded software powerhouse that employs almost 7,000 people worldwide. Revenues for fiscal year 2004 were nearly $1.9 billion, with operating profits of $317 million—an impressive accomplishment in this economic environment. According to Jim Grenier, VP of Total Rewards & Workforce Solutions, Intuit owes a large part of its success to a customer-driven focus from its employees and an almost religious commitment to open management.

A Culture of Employee Satisfaction

Intuit management works hard to ensure that Intuit is "the" company for which people want to work. To get an accurate and candid reading of employee engagement, the company annually administers an anonymous, internal survey of all employees called the "Voice of Employee" survey. In 2003, the results were stunningly positive: 90% of the employees responded, and 82% of them indicated that they would recommend Intuit as an employer to their friends, while 85% said they were proud to work at Intuit. Clearly, Intuit is doing something right when it comes to creating an employee-focused organization.

Employee Ownership Vehicles

All full-time and many part-time employees in North America participate in the company's nonqualified stock option (NSO) plan; this amounts to more than 95% of employees worldwide. As of 2002, all optionees have been subject to a three-year vesting schedule, and new options are granted on a periodic basis determined by a number of factors, including individual performance, turnover, and the need to attract or retain key talent. Because of Intuit's success, the company's optionees have fared much better than those of many other technology firms. Fewer than 30% hold underwater options, and all of those have at least some options that are in the money. Only 20% of all outstanding options are underwater.

Intuit also offers an employee stock purchase plan (ESPP) in which employees can contribute up to 10% of their salary towards the purchase of Intuit shares at a 15% discount. Currently, nearly 50% of worldwide employees are taking advantage of this benefit. There is also a 401(k) plan for which the company matches 150% of the first $1,000 of employee contribution, with an overall match of the greater of 75% of the first 6% an employee contributes or $3,000 per year. Even dating back to before the Enron scandal, Intuit's policy has been to carry none of its own stock in the 401(k) portfolio.

Other Benefits

Intuit offers an array of medical, dental and vision coverage, but there are some unusual benefits as well. Many locations provide "time management services" through local vendors: dry cleaners, oil change, car wash, credit union, and mobile dental care are among those "extras" provided to make life a little easier for the employees.

Shifting the Focus

Intuit has begun to shift its focus away from a core of equity-based compensation in favor of a "total rewards portfolio" comprised of multiple components. This is motivated, in part, by the high historical "run rate" in option grants, resulting in ongoing dilution of shareholder value. Institutions own over 80% of Intuit's stock, and these shareholders have demanded a substantial reduction in dilution, so the company has implemented or partially implemented a number of changes, including:

- Reducing the old 10-year option plan with a 4-year vesting period to a 7-year plan with 3-year vesting
- Reducing a plethora of option pools with manager-level discretion to just one pool allocated by the CEO
- Adding or significantly enhancing incentive plans with bigger cash pools for high performance
- Maintaining emphasis on the ESPP
- Paying more competitive salaries

  Significantly enhancing the 401(k) company match for all participating employees
- A cash and non-cash on-the-spot recognition program with a sizable budget

As a result of these initiatives, the number of net grants annually has been reduced to under 3% of outstanding shares—a figure that is consistent with the ultimate goal of between 2% and 3% net annual dilution. In addition, the company is looking at other means to better balance the equity-to-cash ratio. Performance-based vesting, longer-term cash plans, and restricted stock are all on the table for study and consideration.

Communicating the Message

Steve Bennett, Intuit's CEO, visits most major locations twice each year. He conducts "skip-level" meetings with various employees at all levels, and every quarter he broadcasts a "State of the Business" message to all locations. This is followed up with a live Q&A broadcast to answer employees' questions. The company is very committed to continually building a "line of sight" from each and every employee all the way to the CEO so that no one will be in doubt about the mission or feel disenfranchised by the organization.

Employee Ownership with an Internal Market at TEOCO

Pam Chernoff

Employee ownership has been a cornerstone of the culture at TEOCO since the firm was founded. Fairfax, VA-based TEOCO, an acronym for "The Employee Owned Company," has served its clients since 1995. Over that time, founder, chairman, and CEO Atul Jain has maintained a strong commitment to employee ownership, even as his thinking about some aspects of its structure evolved. TEOCO is 100% owned by current employees, former employees, and members of its board of directors.

TEOCO's main line of business is providing network cost and revenue management solutions for telecom carriers and large enterprise clients. TEOCO also runs an Internet-based service at *www.respond.com,* matching online consumers with local service professionals in the U.S. and Canada. TEOCO grew from revenues of $8 million in 2000 to more than $20 million in 2005, during a time when many technology companies were hanging up their hats. TEOCO has thrived because its key product, cost management software, has been in demand, and because it has continuously adapted to changing times.

Employee Ownership Mechanisms

Until 2000, employees obtained ownership interests by purchasing shares offered to them at book value. That January, due to an increase in the company's book value and cost associated with purchasing the company shares, TEOCO started granting new-hire stock options, a decision that Jain now thinks negatively affected the ownership culture he was trying to build. Although he does not regret the decision, he does think that retaining some elements of the stock purchase program would have been helpful. Share ownership is a more powerful motivator than stock option grants, he states, because people who own shares outright feel a sense of ownership no matter where the stock price is—especially if they've paid for the shares out of their own pockets. As a result, the company is continually looking to put mechanisms in place that put a greater emphasis on stock ownership and less emphasis on stock options. A new mechanism introduced in 2005 enables employees to purchase 100 shares per month through a payroll deduction program. Another mechanism allows employees to take some or all of their cash bonuses in the form of stock grants.

When an employee starts work at TEOCO, he or she is typically granted 2,000 to 10,000 incentive stock options, which, like all of TEOCO's options, vest over four years. In addition, a new employee who meets his or her 90-day goals receives an offer to purchase outright 500 or 1,000 shares. Lately, about 30% of new employees have been purchasing such shares. Employees earn additional options if the company or their line of business meets its financial targets for the year. That system replaced one that stressed individual rather than group performance.

To reward key performers, the company established its "recognition level" program in 2001. Under this program, employees can be promoted to one of three "recognition levels": principal, senior principal, or vice president. No one who takes a job at the company, no matter their accomplishments before they joined TEOCO, starts at a recognition level, because what the person accomplishes there is more important to the company than what they've done in the past. An employee who is promoted through successive levels gets further option grants at the time of promotion. An employee who is promoted to principal gets 8,000 options. A subsequent promotion to senior principal, usually no less than two years later, nets 16,000 options. A promotion to vice president means 32,000 more.

When any employee's most recent grant expires, he or she receives a replacement grant. An employee who has not achieved a recognition level gets 4,000 options; employees at the three recognition levels get 8,000, 16,000, and 32,000, respectively.

Jain counts among his accomplishments the decision to instill an ownership culture from the start and to insist that employees adhere to the company's core values. Those decisions have helped create a powerful culture and have been a good recruitment and retention tool, he states. The decision in 1998 to change the company's name from Strategic Technology Group to TEOCO means that people do not forget the name or what the company stands for. He is also proud of having formed the company's Advisory Team of employee volunteers who make recommendations to the leadership team on such issues as policy, employee concerns, corporate governance, and corporate communications.

The Internal Stock Market

With the help of the Beyster Institute, TEOCO has instituted an internal stock market modeled on one developed at Science Applications International Corporation (SAIC) when SAIC was a private company. All sellers sell to the company, and all buyers buy from the company. To match buyers and sellers in the internal stock market, orders will be fulfilled in increments rather than percentages, meaning that if, say, buyers ask for 1,000, 6,000, and 40,000 shares, but fewer than 47,000 shares are available, the orders will be filled based on size rather than percentage. So everyone will get 1,000, then the remaining two will get another 5,000, and the remainder will go to the person who wanted 40,000.

The plan is administered by a committee appointed by TEOCO's board of directors. Transactions occur once or twice a year on specific trade dates set by the company. On a given trade date, all transactions take place at a preannounced trade price determined by the administrative committee, based on a price range from an independent appraiser. After a trade date and its trade price are announced, the company organizes meetings where participants can ask questions about the company and review its financial statements and valuation report.

Participation is limited to current officers, other employees, and directors, plus former employees, and trusts for the benefit of a current or former employee or immediate family members (if such an employee or family member has more than 50% of the trust's beneficial interest). Otherwise eligible participants will be ineligible to participate on a given trade date if such participation (as determined by the administrative committee) would result in the violation of a law (such as SEC Rule 701) or would involve a breach of fiduciary duty.

The SEC has issued a no-action letter regarding TEOCO's internal market. (A no-action letter is a response to a company's question regarding the legality of a proposed activity under the federal securities laws; it states the SEC will not take enforcement action against that activity under the given circumstances.)

In preparation for launching the internal market, TEOCO shortened the options' lifespan from 10 years from the grant date to 5 years a few years ago. The company also switched from book value to fair market value in October 2003. The company has also relaxed its repurchase rules to allow employees who stayed for at least five years and who have owned their shares outright for at least three years to hang onto them if they leave. The company retains the right of first refusal.

TEOCO is now seriously exploring establishing a non-leveraged employee stock ownership plan (ESOP). The main driver behind evaluating an ESOP is to create a vehicle that gets significant number of shares in the hands of employees on an annual basis. Some of the mechanisms currently in place may change and evolve as a result of implementing an ESOP.

About the Authors

Barbara Baksa is the executive director of the National Association of Stock Plan Professionals (NASPP). She is a Certified Equity Professional (CEP) and serves on the Certified Equity Professional Institute's certification council and the NCEO's board of directors. She is a frequent speaker on equity compensation-related topics and has spoken at NCEO, NASPP, and other industry events. In addition to her speaking engagements, she has authored several white papers on equity compensation-related topics and has contributed chapters to four books on equity compensation.

Pam Chernoff is the director of equity compensation projects at the National Center for Employee Ownership (NCEO). She is a Certified Equity Professional (CEP) and the editor of *The Stock Options Book* and the NCEO's online Equity Compensation Basics course and annual Equity Compensation Updates.

Paul Davis is the president of the Scanlon Leadership Network, a nonprofit association that promotes the Scanlon principles, provides networking opportunities for members, serves as a clearinghouse of Scanlon information, and supplies Scanlon-related products and services.

Bryan Girard was formerly NCEO's director of communications.

Cathy Ivancic is a consultant for and co-owner of Workplace Development Inc. Since 1985, she has helped more than 100 ESOP companies enhance ESOP communications and develop an ownership culture. She is active in national organizations that promote shared ownership.

Neil N. Koenig is a Fresno, California-based family business and management consultant.

Jerry McAdams is the national practice leader for reward and recognition systems at Watson Wyatt Worldwide.

Bill Nicholson is a CPA active in the ESOP community.

Darryl Orr wrote his chapter when he was chief operations officer at Smith & Company. He is a registered professional engineer and has owned and operated consulting engineering firms since 1971.

Corey Rosen is the executive director of the National Center for Employee Ownership (NCEO). He received his Ph.D. from Cornell University in political science in 1973, taught government at Ripon College until 1976, and then served as a Senate staff member until 1981, when he cofounded the NCEO.

Jack Stack is the president and CEO of SRC Holdings Corporation.

Matt Ward is a senior vice president of technology compensation consulting at the Radford Surveys unit of Aon Consulting. He has more than 20 years of consulting experience, with a focus on strategic annual and long-term incentive plan design for both publicly traded and private companies. Before joining Aon Consulting, Matt was founder/CEO of WestWard Pay Strategies, Inc. in San Francisco. Matt is an attorney and CPA.

Fred Whittlesey is the founding principal of Compensation Venture Group (CVG) and serves as chief compensation officer of PayScale, Inc. He has an extensive compensation consulting background and corporate compensation experience. Before founding CVG, he was the senior vice president of Aon Consulting/Radford Surveys and prior to that held corporate compensation positions at Broadcom and Amazon.com.

About the NCEO

The National Center for Employee Ownership (NCEO) is widely considered to be the leading authority in employee ownership in the U.S. and the world. Established in 1981 as a nonprofit information and membership organization, it now has over 2,500 members, including companies, professionals, unions, government officials, academics, and interested individuals. It is funded entirely through the work it does.

The NCEO's mission is to provide the most objective, reliable information possible about employee ownership at the most affordable price possible. As part of the NCEO's commitment to providing objective information, it does not lobby or provide ongoing consulting services. The NCEO publishes a variety of materials on employee ownership and participation, holds dozens of seminars, Webinars, and conferences on employee ownership annually, and offers a variety of online courses. The NCEO's work includes extensive contacts with the media, both through articles written for trade and professional publications and through interviews with reporters. It has written or edited five books for outside publishers during the past two decades. Finally, the NCEO maintains an extensive Web site at *www.nceo.org*.

See the following page for information on membership benefits and fees.

Membership Benefits

NCEO members receive the following benefits:

- The bimonthly newsletter, *Employee Ownership Report*, which covers ESOPs, stock options, and employee participation.
- Access to the members-only area of the NCEO's Web site, which includes online tools such as a searchable database of over 200 NCEO members who are service providers in this field, a searchable archive of newsletters, and more.
- Substantial discounts on publications and events produced by the NCEO (such as this book).
- The right to telephone the NCEO for answers to general or specific questions regarding employee ownership.

An introductory NCEO membership costs $80 for one year ($90 outside the U.S.) and covers an entire company at all locations, a single professional offering services in this field, or a single individual with a business interest in employee ownership. Full-time students and faculty members who are not employed in the business sector may join at the academic rate of $35 for one year ($45 outside the U.S.).

Selected NCEO Publications on Employee Ownership and Participation

The NCEO offers a variety of publications on all aspects of employee ownership and participation. Following are descriptions of some of our main publications in these areas. We publish new books and revise old ones on a yearly basis. To obtain the most current information on what we have available, visit our extensive Web site at *www.nceo.org* or call us at 510-208-1300.

Equity Compensation

- This book, *Incentive Compensation and Employee Ownership*, takes a broad look at how companies can use incentives, ranging from stock plans to cash bonuses to gainsharing, to motivate and reward employees. It includes both technical discussions and case studies.

$25 for NCEO members, $35 for nonmembers

- *The Stock Options Book* is a straightforward, comprehensive overview covering the legal, accounting, regulatory, and design issues involved in implementing a stock option or stock purchase plan. It is our main book on the subject and possibly the most popular book in the field.

   $25 for NCEO members, $35 for nonmembers

- *Selected Issues in Equity Compensation* is more detailed and specialized than *The Stock Options Book*, with chapters on issues such as repricing, securities issues, and evergreen options.

   $25 for NCEO members, $35 for nonmembers

- *Beyond Stock Options* is a guide to phantom stock, stock appreciation rights, restricted stock, direct stock purchase plans, and performance awards used as alternatives to stock options. It includes a CD with plan documents.

   $35 for NCEO members, $50 for nonmembers

- *Accounting for Equity Compensation* is a guide to the financial accounting rules that govern equity compensation programs in the United States.

   $35 for NCEO members, $50 for nonmembers

- *The Stock Administration Book* is a comprehensive guide to administering stock options and other equity compensation plans. It includes a CD with templates for immediate use.

   $50 for NCEO members, $75 for nonmembers

- *Equity Compensation in a Post-Expensing World* is a collection of essays on strategies for choosing and structuring equity compensation plans when expensing is required.

   $25 for NCEO members, $35 for nonmembers

- *Employee Stock Purchase Plans* covers how ESPPs work, tax and legal issues, administration, accounting, communicating the plan to employees, and research on what companies are doing with their plans.

  $25 for NCEO members, $35 for nonmembers

- *Equity-Based Compensation for Multinational Corporations* describes how companies can use stock options and other equity-based programs across the world to reward a global work force. It includes a country-by-country summary of tax and legal issues as well as a detailed case study.

  $25 for NCEO members, $35 for nonmembers

- *Tax and Securities Sources for Equity Compensation* contains selected primary source materials such as statutes.

  $35 for NCEO members, $50 for nonmembers

Employee Stock Ownership Plans (ESOPs)

- *The ESOP Reader* is an overview of the issues involved in establishing and operating an ESOP. It covers the basics of ESOP rules, feasibility, valuation, and other matters, and then discusses managing an ESOP company, including brief case studies. The book is intended for those with a general interest in ESOPs and employee participation.

  $25 for NCEO members, $35 for nonmembers

- *Selling to an ESOP* is a guide for owners, managers, and advisors of closely held businesses. It explains how ESOPs work and then offers a comprehensive look at legal structures, valuation, financing (including self-financing), and other matters, especially the tax-deferred section 1042 "rollover" that allows owners to indefinitely defer capital gains taxation on the proceeds of the sale to the ESOP.

  $25 for NCEO members, $35 for nonmembers

- *Leveraged ESOPs and Employee Buyouts* discusses how ESOPs borrow money to buy out entire companies, purchase shares from a retiring owner, or finance new capital. Beginning with a primer on leveraged ESOPs and their uses, it then discusses contribution limits, valuation, accounting, feasibility studies, financing sources, and more.

    $25 for NCEO members, $35 for nonmembers

- The *Model ESOP* contains a sample ESOP plan, with alternative provisions given to tailor the plan to individual needs. It also includes a section-by-section explanation of the plan and other supporting materials.

    $50 for NCEO members, $75 for nonmembers

- *ESOP Valuation* brings together and updates where needed the best articles on ESOP valuation that we have published in our *Journal of Employee Ownership Law and Finance,* described below.

    $25 for NCEO members, $35 for nonmembers

- *ESOPs and Corporate Governance* covers everything from shareholder rights to the impact of Sarbanes-Oxley to choosing a fiduciary.

    $25 for NCEO members, $35 for nonmembers

- The *ESOP Communications Sourcebook* provides ideas for and examples of communicating an ESOP to employees and customers. It includes a CD with communications materials, including many documents that readers can customize for their own companies.

    $35 for NCEO members, $50 for nonmembers

- *Executive Compensation in ESOP Companies* discusses executive compensation issues, special ESOP considerations, and the first-ever survey of executive compensation in ESOP companies.

    $25 for NCEO members, $35 for nonmembers

- *S Corporation ESOPs* introduces the reader to how ESOPs work and then discusses the legal, valuation, administrative, and other issues associated with S corporation ESOPs.

  $25 for NCEO members, $35 for nonmembers

- *The ESOP Committee Guide* describes the different types of ESOP committees, the range of goals they can address, alternative structures, member selection criteria, training, committee life cycle concerns, and other issues.

  $25 for NCEO members, $35 for nonmembers

- *Wealth and Income Consequences of Employee Ownership* is a detailed report on a comparative study of ESOP companies in Washington State that found ESOP companies pay more and provided better benefits than other companies.

  $10 for NCEO members, $15 for nonmembers

- *How ESOP Companies Handle the Repurchase Obligation* includes both essays and research on the subject.

  $25 for NCEO members, $35 for nonmembers

Employee Involvement and Management

- *Front Line Finance Facilitator's Manual* gives step-by-step instructions for teaching business literacy, emphasizing ESOPs.

  $50 for NCEO members, $75 for nonmembers

- *Front Line Finance Diskette* contains the workbook for participants in electronic form (so a copy can be printed out for everyone) in the *Front Line Finance* course.

  $50 for NCEO members, $75 for nonmembers

- *Ownership Management* draws upon the experience of the NCEO and of leading employee ownership companies to discuss how to build a culture of lasting innovation by combining employee ownership with employee involvement programs.

  $25 for NCEO members, $35 for nonmembers

Other

- *Section 401(k) Plans and Employee Ownership* focuses on how company stock is used in 401(k) plans, both in stand-alone 401(k) plans and combination 401(k)–ESOP plans ("KSOPs").

  $25 for NCEO members, $35 for nonmembers

- *The Journal of Employee Ownership Law and Finance* is the only professional journal solely devoted to employee ownership. Articles are written by leading experts and cover ESOPs, stock options, and related subjects in depth.

  One-year subscription (four issues):
  $75 for NCEO members, $100 for nonmembers

To join the NCEO as a member or to order any of the publications listed here, use the order form on the following page, use the secure ordering system on our Web site at www.nceo.org, or call us at 510-208-1300. If you join at the same time you order publications, you will receive the members-only publication discounts.

Order Form

To order, fill out this form and mail it with your credit card information or check to the NCEO at 1736 Franklin St., 8th Flr., Oakland, CA 94612; fax it with your credit card information to the NCEO at 510-272-9510; telephone us at 510-208-1300 with your credit card in hand; or order securely online at our Web site, *www.nceo.org.* If you are not already a member, you can join now to receive member discounts on the publications you order.

Name

Organization

Address

City, State, Zip (Country)

Telephone   Fax   E-mail

Method of Payment: ❑ Check (payable to "NCEO")   ❑ Visa   ❑ M/C   ❑ AMEX

Credit Card Number

Signature   Exp. Date

Checks are accepted only for orders from the U.S. and must be in U.S. currency.

Title	Qty.	Price	Total

Tax: California residents add 8.25% sales tax (on publications only, not membership or Journal subscriptions)

Shipping: In the U.S., first publication $5, each add'l $1; outside the U.S., we charge exact shipping costs to your credit card, plus a $10 handling surcharge; no shipping charges for memberships or Journal subscriptions

Introductory NCEO Membership: $80 for one year ($90 outside the U.S.)

Subtotal	$
Sales Tax	$
Shipping	$
Membership	$
TOTAL DUE	$